CHANTRY CHAPEL TO ROYAL GRAMMAR SCHOOL

The History of Kingston Grammar School

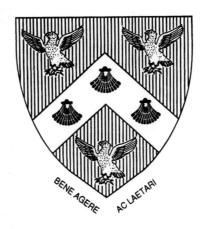

BENE AGERE AC LAETARI

CHANTRY CHAPEL
TO
ROYAL GRAMMAR SCHOOL

—··◆··—

THE HISTORY OF
Kingston Grammar School

—··◆··—

David Ward and Gordon Evans

GRESHAM BOOKS LIMITED
in partnership with
KINGSTON GRAMMAR SCHOOL

© Kingston Grammar School 2000

Published by
Gresham Books Limited
The Gresham Press
46 Victoria Road
Summertown
Oxford
OX2 7QD

In partnership with
Kingston Grammar School
70 London Road
Kingston upon Thames
Surrey
KT2 6PY

ISBN 0 946095 36 1

Design and typesetting by John Saunders Design and Production
Jacket design by Brian Melville
Printed and bound by MPG Books Ltd, Cornwall

Contents

—··◆··—

Foreword

—··◆··—

This book, authorised by the Governing Body in 1994, could not have seen the light of day without the help of a great many people. Many staff and Old Kingstonians have assisted; and no less than five Headmasters have been involved – Duncan Baxter, Tony Creber, Sidney Miller, John Strover, and, before his death in 1998, Percy Rundle. Then there are those who over the years have maintained the records without which the School story could hardly be traced at all; the compilers of the School's annual accounts (1674 onwards), the Secretaries of the Governing Bodies (1872 onwards) and of course over 117 years the Editors of the School Magazine. Outside the School community, from 1860 onwards the *Surrey Comet* has covered the School's activities and provided an invaluable source of information.

We had valuable assistance from Leicester Museum who provided a copy of the 1585 National Appeal for a new set of school buildings and from Hampshire County Record Office who located a previously unknown petition to the Bishop of Winchester from a disgruntled Master, in 1725. June Sampson whose work on the history of Kingston is so well known and respected passed on useful advice at the outset of the project on where to locate sources; and Tim Everson, Local History Officer for Kingston upon Thames gave freely of his time answering queries and locating documents. He also discovered the existence of a previously unknown 17th century Master, albeit one whose term of office only lasted a year or so.

To all of these people we owe our thanks but of course they are not responsible for any errors or omissions. These all rest with the two of us, Gordon Evans being responsible for Chapters 13 to 15 on the sporting history of the School, and David Ward for the earlier Chapters. Whatever its imperfections our book does break new ground for there has never before been a full-scale history of Kingston Grammar School. In the early 50s R H James, Senior History Master prepared a study of the School, which majored on the medieval period. But it was never published. M C Cowan, a sixth former, wrote half a dozen well-researched articles on the School's history for the

Kingstonian in 1953-1955. And finally, Percy Rundle when Head prepared a brief memoir on the School and its origins in 1961 when the Queen came to celebrate the 400ᵗʰ anniversary of its foundation by Elizabeth I in 1561. So it was clearly time to fill the gap.

To Mrs Helena Smith of the School staff we are also particularly grateful. Getting the text into a fit state for it to go to the publishers, Gresham Books, was a big job done efficiently and with unfailing good humour. And finally we must thank our wives who had to put up with the disruptions the project caused, over several years, to our domestic lives. Their patience and support were so important.

DAVID WARD and GORDON EVANS

Reverend David Ward, M A was at Kingston Grammar School from 1943 to 1951,. and went on to St John's College, Cambridge where he obtained a First in History. After National Service he joined the Civil Service, becoming an Under-Secretary in DHSS before changing careers at 50 to become a clergyman. He was Vicar of Immanuel, Streatham Common till 1987 and then locally of St Paul's, Hook till 1993. A governor of the School, he is also a member of the Old Kingstonian Association Committee.

G W Evans, B A an Old Boy of the School (1936–1944), joined the staff of Kingston Grammar School in 1950 on leaving New College, Oxford where he read History and subsequently took a Diploma in Education. He was for many years Senior History Master, and was Master in Charge of Cricket for a time in the 1970s. He retired in 1987 having been Second Master for fourteen years. He played hockey for Wales in the 1950s and helped to run the Welsh Schoolboys' Eleven between 1970 and 1980.

Preface

—··◆··—

The academic year 1999-2000 not only sees Kingston Grammar School enter the new millennium, but is also the year when we celebrate the 700th anniversary of the wedding feast prepared on the 16th September 1299 by Edward Lovekyn for Edward 1 which led to the building of the Chapel of St Mary Magdelene, and ultimately to the foundation of Queen Elizabeth's Grammar School in 1561. It is most timely, therefore, that this school history should be published in 2000.

A new Information and Communication Technology Centre, together with a Multi-Media Modern Language Centre, are the latest additions to the school which has evolved from a small Elizabethan Grammar School, to a Direct Grant Grammar School and is now a thriving independent co-educational school with over 600 pupils. However, any school is much more than its site and facilities, more even than its traditions. Essentially it is *people* who are the school – pupils, staff, parents, governors, benefactors and past pupils. David Ward and Gordon Evans chart the progress of Kingston Grammar School from its humble origins by showing how individuals have met challenges, seized opportunities and recovered from setbacks.

That the school can face the 21st Century with confidence derives from the strengths we have inherited from the past, and the willingness of each generation to look forward. We are hugely indebted to the authors and all who have assisted in the production of this history for reminding us of our inheritance, and for providing such a fascinating insight into the history of education in Kingston.

DUNCAN BAXTER
HEADMASTER

CHAPEL AND SCHOOL
DAVID WARD

CHAPTER 1

—··◆··—

Beginnings

—··◆··—

IF YOU STAND AT THE WINDOW in the School Library and look out across London Road you will see, immediately opposite the School, a modest chapel. It is quite inconspicuous, occupying a small site at the very corner of the busy junction where Queen Elizabeth Road joins London Road. Its importance is far from obvious, yet this is a starred Grade 2 Listed monument. It is by far the oldest complete building in Kingston upon Thames. It is the only surviving free-standing chantry chapel in England, dating from 1309. Its endowments provided in large part the endowments for the Elizabethan foundation of the School, and with its outbuildings, this chapel housed the whole school from Elizabethan times up to 1878, continuing to be used as a teaching area until 1992. To this day the chapel belongs solely to the School as part of its freehold. So any history to the School must start with the story of the chapel.

The Foundation of the Lovekyn Chapel

Edward Lovekyn, who founded the chapel, was born in Kingston in 1239 of a well established local family. He was a caterer by trade and like other members of his family belonged to the Company of Butchers of Kingston upon Thames (which included all bakers, confectioners and provision merchants as well as butchers). He was Bailiff of Kingston in 1277 and again in 1284. A citizen of London from 1292 he had houses in Billingsgate, and at Bridge-foot in Kingston.

In the year 1299 King Edward I twice visited the town, on 23rd February and 8th March. He was entertained to meals provided by Edward Lovekyn. The King was so impressed with the hospitality that he asked Edward, with his son Robert, to provide the catering for the marriage feast at his forthcoming wedding to Princess Margaret of France. This was the sort of request it would have been most unwise to refuse, and so, on 16th September 1299, the Lovekyns laid on the wedding feast. Whilst the King expressed himself greatly pleased, he was in no hurry to pay the bill; and when he died in 1307,

The 14th Century Chantry Chapel of St Mary Magdalene : Lovekyn's Chapel

whilst some payments had been made on account, 1000 marks (a mark was worth 13s 4d) was still owing. The scale of this debt can be measured by the fact that in the 13th century beef was 4lbs for a penny; whilst a labourer earned 2d a day, and a carpenter 3d. The new King, Edward II, inherited the debt, but there was no reason to think he would be in any more hurry than his father to clear the bill.

It was now that Edward Lovekyn approached the Crown with a proposition. If the King would grant him a licence to found and endow a chantry chapel at Kingston, he would cancel the entire debt, save for a nominal 100 shillings. Edward II agreed the deal.

So what was a chantry chapel? It was one built, endowed and consecrated as a chapel in which its appointed priest, or priests, said prayers and masses for the repose of the souls of its pious founder and members of his family after their death. It was not intended, or allowed, to be used for congregational or even family worship. It was illegal under the Statute of Mortmain to found such a chapel without the express permission of the Crown. Most of the chantry chapels were attached to major churches. Separate chapels like the one Edward Lovekyn wanted to found were the exception, and disliked by the parochial clergy who wanted to see local wealth devoted to their own places of worship not "squandered" in chantries.

It may be that piety moved Edward, but there is no doubt the status of the

Lovekyn family could only have been enhanced by the foundation of their own chapel at Norbiton, on the London Road. By Letters Patent dated 11th June 1309 it was stated:

"Edward Lovekyn, townsman of Kingston may assign and grant ten acres of land and one acre of meadow and 5 marks of rent with appurtenances to the certain chaplain to celebrate mass daily in the Chapel of the Blessed Mary Magdalene in Kingston for the souls of all the departed faithful."

A few weeks later came the Episcopal Licence of the Bishop of Winchester on 19th July 1309. This authorised Edward and his heirs to

"appoint a suitable chaplain canonically inducted by us and our successors and sufficiently endowed by you and your successors in the chapel recently constructed by you in honour of the Blessed Mary Magdalene within the parish boundaries of the church of Kingston for the performance of Divine Service and the celebration there for the souls of the departed but so that no prejudice may arise therefrom to the mother church and the rector and vicar thereof."

The chaplain, whose salary would be met from the endowment, was to reside in the manse adjoining the chapel. And so all was ready for the installation of the first chaplain, Ralph de Stanle, on 23rd March 1310. Just 4 months later on 27th July, Edward Lovekyn died leaving two sons, Robert and John. Unfortunately Robert did not seem as interested in the chantry chapel as his father might have wished. Shortly after Edward's death complaints were made that Robert had withheld the endowments of the Chapel and in 1312 he was excommunicated; but he was clearly readmitted to the fold, for in 1327 Archbishop Reynolds wrote to the Bishop of Winchester telling him to take action to stop Robert diverting Chantry rents "by reason of which the sustention of the chaplain celebrating Divine Service there has ceased". Robert died in 1330.

John Lovekyn Restores the Chapel

The new Chapel continued to have a troubled time. There were disputes with the Vicar of Kingston over finances, and matters came to a head in 1347 when the Bishop of Winchester wrote to the Dean of Ewell to say that he had heard that the Chaplain, Walter Couke of Fenistratford, was non-resident. Worse, he *"has audaciously applied as his own the rents and pervenients of the Chapel, and left it almost destitute of Divine Services ..."* The Dean is to ensure the Chaplain returns to his duties, and repairs the edifice of the Chapel *"which is clearly in impending ruin."*

Fortunately help came in the person of John Lovekyn, Edward's son by his second wife Isabel, who had only been a child when the Chapel was founded. He had become a stock-fishmonger, or purveyor of dried fish, an important part of everyone's diet in those days. His business, in London, had flourished.

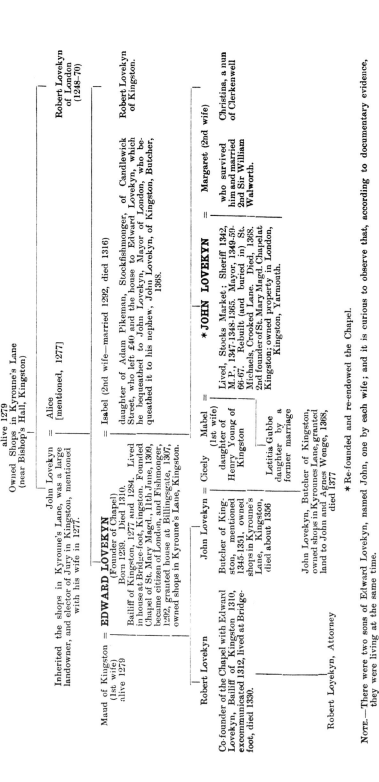

NOTE.—There were two sons of Edward Lovekyn, named John, one by each wife; and it is curious to observe that, according to documentary evidence, they were living at the same time.

The Lovekyn family in the time of the Chapel's foundation.

(Prepared by Dr Finny)

4

He was a City Alderman, Sheriff of London in 1342, a Member of Parliament, a Privy Councillor and four times Lord Mayor of London. He owned quays in London, Yarmouth and Gorleston, and had a fleet of ships trading with the Continent in fish, coal, and general merchandise. He was a man of such substance that he was able to contribute £200 towards the King's expedition to France in 1338.

John Lovekyn's first term as Lord Mayor coincided with the arrival in London of the Black Death, probably bubonic plague. There was no known cure, thousands upon thousands died, and indeed over the period up to 1370 it has been estimated that perhaps 1.5 million people died – a third of the population of England. Many people's thoughts turned to religion and it seems that John was no exception. He decided to re-endow the Lovekyn Chapel and did so in a munificent way. The building was restored, under licence from King Edward III in 1352, and in 1355 John increased the endowments of the Chapel with 250 acres of land, 9 houses and 10 shops in Kingston, and the rents of two houses in London. From then on the Chapel had two chaplains, the senior one called the Custos (warden).

Detailed rules were laid down for the conduct of the many services – which were not to conflict with those at the Parish Church. These included a daily mass for the souls of the Lovekyn family – and at grace after dinner they were to be remembered again with the words, *"May the souls of John, Edward and Robert Lovekyn our founders, and of William Lord Bishop of Winchester and of all other faithful people deceased, through the mercy of God rest in peace."* The chaplains were to go to the Church four times a year *"and make their offerings"*. No parishioner was to be present at any sacrament in the Chapel excepting John Lovekyn himself. But the key to peace breaking out between Church and Chapel was that John Lovekyn gave a house to the Vicar, near the Bridge, to belong to the Vicar for the time being, for ever. *"In return for this so great bounty"*, the Concordat stated the Custos and chaplains *"should have and retain all and singular the oblations arising at the said chapel, to be by them applied to their own sole and proper uses, without any let or molestation of the Vicar whatsoever."*

Everyone signed up! The Bishop of Winchester, the Dean and the Chapter of the Cathedral, the Prior of Merton (Patrons of the Parish Church), the Vicar of Kingston, and John Lovekyn himself.

William Walworth's Benefaction

There was to be one more great benefactor in the 14th century. John Lovekyn had as his apprentice a young man called William Walworth who after John's death in 1368 took over his business, and married his widow, Margaret. He was Lord Mayor in 1373 and again in 1379. His claim to fame is that during his second term of office he and his entourage slew Wat Tyler, leader of the Peasants' Revolt, outside the walls of the city, for which the King awarded

Sir William Walworth Lord Mayor of London 1373 and 1379, a generous benefactor

Lovekyn Chapel : 14th Century bracket representing Edward III

him a Knighthood and a substantial pension. No doubt because of the family connection William gave much to the Lovekyn Chapel. In a grant of 1371 he conveyed to the Custos a mill, a dovecote, 150 acres of land (arable, meadow, pasture and woodland) and the rents of various properties. He specified that there should be a third chaplain.

From this time on until the reign of Henry VIII there was a continuous succession of Wardens (Custos) and chaplains appointed by the Bishop of Winchester, serving as Chantry priests, conducting Divine Services and maintaining the structure of the Chapel and its outbuildings. We have the names and dates of most of these Wardens but nothing else. Their establishment was a great deal more than the Chapel building itself. By the 16th century there were as well:

"1. A garden adjoining on the East. 2. A small chapel called St Ann's adjoining to the former with a Chamber and Study over it. 3. One other inner Chamber and an Hawk's Mew over it. 4. A small Chapel called St Loyes on the south side of Mary Magdalene's with a little place under it. 5. An old kitchen, with a Chamber adjoining it and a Solarium or loft over both. 6. A Chamber under the said kitchen on the west side of Mary Magdalene's Chapel beyond the footway leading to London. 7. An house next to the said kitchen. 8. A yard on the North side of Mary Magdalene's Chapel and another on the West side thereof. 9. A gallery over the said yards leading from the Chamber over St Ann's Chapel to a small place and to two Chambers called the Masters Lodgings. 10. One Cellar and four small

Chambers under the Masters Lodgings. 11. One end of a Granary, with a partition at the West end from the old Granary. 12. A Stable at the West end of the said Granary, and a Dovecote."

Letters Patent 26th April 1547
leasing the property to Richard
Taverner.

It was this property which was to become the seat of the Grammar School in due course. But meantime, what of schooling in Kingston during medieval times?

Schooling in Medieval Kingston

Commending an Appeal for funds to preserve the Lovekyn Chapel, in 1921, the Headmaster and the Mayor of Kingston wrote that

"there had been a School connected with the Chantry since its foundation in 1309, but Henry VIII suppressed it, in common with all such foundations, and it was in abeyance until 1561 when Queen Elizabeth gave it to the Grammar School which she had endowed."

There is an element of wishful thinking in this very positive statement, for there really are two separate questions. The first is this: is there evidence of what one might call secondary education, up to 14 or 15 years of age, during the three centuries before the founding of the Grammar School? The second question is whether, if there was such schooling, it was at any time linked to the Chapel and its chaplains?

It is a reasonable assumption that there would have been schooling, beyond primary stage, in the town. It was a thriving market town, 11 miles from the City, on the main London to Portsmouth road, and on the banks of a major commercial highway – the River Thames. The first of many town charters was granted by King John in 1200 and amongst the most important thereafter were those confirming 8-day fairs on All Souls' Day, by Henry III, and at Whitsun by Edward III. But the jewel in Kingston's crown was of course the Bridge, the first upstream all the way from London Bridge itself.

Moreover there is just a little documentary evidence of a school or schools in Kingston.

The first is a document relating to a lawsuit in 1272 concerning the ownership of lands in Marsh fields. It refers to a certain Master Gilbert de Suthewelle, Rector of the Schools at Kingston. The terms Master and Rector indicate that the establishment must have been a significant one, but no more is known of it.

The second document is rather more revealing. It is a letter from the Bishop of Winchester to the Prior of the Cathedral monastery at Canterbury asking him to return the belongings of Hugh of Kingston. The Prior had them

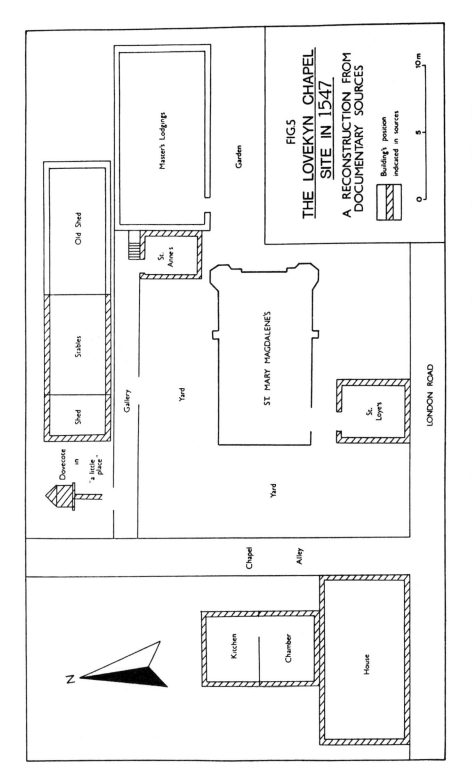

FIG.5
THE LOVEKYN CHAPEL
SITE IN 1547
A RECONSTRUCTION FROM
DOCUMENTARY SOURCES

Building's position
indicated in sources

0   5   10m

N

Master's Lodgings

Garden

Old Shed

Stables

Shed

St. Anne's

Gallery

Yard

ST MARY MAGDALENE'S

Dovecote
in
"a little
place"

Yard

St. Loye's

LONDON ROAD

Chapel

Alley

Kitchen

Chamber

House

The Chapel and associated buildings, listed in the Letters Patent 1547 when the whole property was leased to Richard Taverner

9

seized when Hugh decided to change schools, moving from Canterbury to Kingston. Hugh had responded to a call from the parishioners *"they to their grief being without a teacher or master of their boys, and others coming to the said town, where a school has been accustomed to be kept."* A contract had been signed for Hugh to take up his post at Michaelmas 1363. In April 1364, when the letter was written, he was still trying to get hold of his belongings from his old school! The letter specifically states that Hugh was to *"undertake the instruction and teaching of the said boys and of other scholars in the said town and preside over the Public School there."*

So at that time there was a school of some consequence in the town. It was well established; it attracted students from beyond the town itself; Hugh came from what was already a well known school at the Almonry, Canterbury; and Kingston's school was called a Public School, i.e. one open to the public without restriction. One can see why the parishioners valued it so highly. Sadly Kingston's own official medieval records are scanty, and add nothing.

Thirdly there is a passing reference in the Kingston Churchwardens' Account book for the year 1504, which states that the wardens had sold some wood to *"John Starkey, Sargent of ye skolars of our Soveren Lord ye King"*.

And finally, there is one negative piece of evidence. In 1377 the Vicar of Kingston was instructed to teach his choirboys the rudiments of Latin, but only *"up to Donatus"*, that is, up to a certain elementary standard. He was forbidden to go beyond this. The inference is that there may have been another school in the town, which would deal with more advanced education – perhaps that whose Master was Hugh of Kingston.

Did the school in Kingston have a continuing life through the years from 1272 onwards? No one knows. Was it in any way connected with the Chantry Chapel? Some people in the past have been persuaded it was, drawing on the scanty evidence outlined above and making the point that at least some of the chantry chapels did have an educational function. But against this, there is no direct or indirect reference associating Lovekyn's foundation with teaching of any sort. John Lovekyn's *"Rules for the conduct of Chapel"* go into great detail (even to the fact that visitors to the chaplains' house must pay threepence for their dinner), but do not touch on education; and the description of the buildings in 1547, mentioned earlier, says nothing of a schoolroom. The conclusion must surely be that Kingston did have its school, probably quite a significant one, but there is no evidence to link the school with Lovekyn's Chapel and its chaplains.

CHAPTER 2

—··◆··—

Queen Elizabeth's School

—··◆··—

Last Days of the Chantry Chapel

FOR NEARLY 200 YEARS after its re-foundation by John Lovekyn a succession of Wardens and assistant chaplains maintained the daily worship of the Chapel, conducting masses and praying for the souls of the faithful departed, particularly of course, the souls of the Lovekyn and Walworth families. Most chantry chapels went out with a whimper when they were abolished in 1547 under the Chantries Act of Edward VI, successor to Henry VIII who had earlier dissolved all the monastic establishments. Lovekyn's Chapel however never recovered from an event in 1540, when its Warden was executed.

Charles Carew was the Warden, and Rector of Beddington as well. It seems he was the son of Sir Nicholas Carew, one of Henry VIII's courtiers and Ambassador to the French Court. In 1539 Sir Nicholas made the fatal mistake of backing an unsuccessful rebellion against the King led by the Marquess of Exeter and was executed in 1539. As for Charles he seems to have been no loving son, as he proceeded to rob his widowed mother. The Act of Attainder under which he was charged stated that he had *"with divers others commited an abominable robbery, and with great violence spoiled and robbed Maud Carew, widow, to her utter undoing, which robbery the said Charles has confessed"*.

Fortunately, Sir Nicholas' widow recovered all her money, plate and rings, except for £6 already spent by the robbers. However that did not save Charles Carew who was executed on 12th March 1540. No further Warden was appointed, but at least one chaplain continued in post. John Debenham, Clerk, was still there and received an annual salary of £6-13-4d in 1546-47. Like other chantry chaplains, he was simply pensioned off under the Chantries Act and is recorded, in 1548, as receiving a pension of £5 a year.

A principal purpose of dissolving the chantries was, of course, to raise funds for the Crown. Both properties and endowments fell to be disposed of and in this respect the Lovekyn Chapel was particularly fortunate. Some lands

A detail from "The Armada Portrait" of Queen Elizabeth I by George Gower

and properties had been sold off in 1545 as a result of the forfeiture of Charles Carew, to Robert Lockwood, a clothier of London for £92-18-4d. But the largest part of the property, including the Chapel, was let on a 21 year lease by Edward VI in 1547 to Richard Taverner, one of his Court favourites, for a yearly rental of £12-12d.

Richard Taverner (1505-1575) – the Third Great Benefactor?

Born at the beginning of the 16th century, Richard Taverner was a student at both Oxford and Cambridge. He obtained a Master of Arts degree and then went to work for Cardinal Wolsey. After Wolsey's fall he allied himself with Thomas Cromwell for whom he wrote several works supporting the Reformation. In 1539 he published his most important work – a translation of the whole Bible. This was the first complete Bible to be printed in England. Earlier versions had all been printed on the Continent. He found himself in the Tower in 1541 when Thomas Cromwell fell out of favour. He managed to make his peace with Henry VIII and became a great favourite with the young Edward VI, being granted a licence in 1552 to preach in any place in the King's dominions – even though he was a layman. He translated Erasmus, became High Sheriff of Oxfordshire and more importantly for Kingston, received not only the larger part of the Chapel endowments but also the Bishop of Winchester's Hall in the town (on the site of the "Bishop Out of Residence" pub today) and Norbiton Hall (demolished in 1934). However, though Richard Taverner along with Lovekyn, Walworth and Queen Elizabeth, is one of the four names permanently commemorated in the titles of the School Houses, it is not at all clear why he has always been regarded as a benefactor! Admittedly he surrendered his lease on Chapel lands early so they could be made part of the new school's endowment, but this was no major sacrifice. Perhaps more likely, though it is only supposition, he used his influence at the court of Queen Elizabeth to support the petition for the establishment of a Grammar School in the town.

Towards a Grammar School for Kingston

We simply do not know if the medieval school or schools survived into the 16th century, or if they did, in what form. What we do know is that there were three attempts to found a grammar school, the last of which was successful when Queen Elizabeth granted her Charter in 1561.

In 1528 a certain Isabel Rothewood of London, widow of a girdle-maker, left two tenements with their gardens in Kingston to provide for a school. To be more precise *"to the use mayntenaunce, and supportaction of such a free schole as shall be purchased, obteyned and gotten in Kingston within three years next after my deceas"*. The Will was proved on 11th May 1528, but whether the school was ever established is not known. Isabel's Will provided that if action was not

13

taken within the three year time limit the property was to go to the Universities of Oxford and Cambridge.

We know of the second attempt from the Will of Robert Hammond, the founder of Hampton School. By his Will of 1557, proved on 15th June, he required that his daughter, Jane

"shall pay yerely during the term of 21 yeres next following after my decease unto the Baylifs and freemen of Kingston £6-13-4d to the intent that therewith the said Baylifs and Freemen shall within two hole yeres next after my decese erecte and sett upp a Free Grammar Scole in the said towne of Kyngeston to contynue for evermore, or ells I will that my said daugher shall not paye the said money nor any parte thereof".

Again we do not know whether this provision of Robert Hammond's Will was ever implemented in full, but interestingly his widow, in her Will of 1559 left a small legacy to *"Edmunde Green, Scholemaster of the freegrammer scole of Kingston upon Temys"*.

And so we come to the petition in 1561 by the Bailiffs of Kingston to the Crown for the provision of a royally incorporated and endowed free grammar school. As it happened, two of the executors of Robert Hammond's Will were the Bailiffs that year. In an article for the school magazine, the *Kingstonian* of April 1953, Michael Cowan makes an intriguing suggestion: these Bailiffs, Messrs Snelling and Matson, will have been more aware than most people that the payments under the Will were for 21 years only. At the end of that period the responsibility for funding the school was going to fall on the burgesses of Kingston. That was not an encouraging prospect. So perhaps they decided that in their year of office they would secure the future.

Queen Elizabeth's Foundation, 1561

Sealed on 1st March 1561, Her Majesty's first grant by Letters Patent stated in its preamble:

"henceforth there be and shall be a grammar school to endure for ever in the said town of Kyngeston-upon-Thames which shall be called the free grammar school of Queen Elizabeth, for the education training and instruction of boys and youths in grammar".

Much of the document is concerned with formalities and with the new school being given possession of the Lovekyn Chapel and all the other Chantry buildings on the London Road site. On the management of the school itself the two town Bailiffs for the time being were to be the governors of the possessions, revenues, and goods of the School. The first governors were to be William Matson and George Snelling. Moreover these governors, with the advice of the Bishop of Winchester, were to nominate the Master and Undermaster (also known as usher), to settle their salaries and deal with the

The founding
Charter of 1st
March 1561

15

Photo of mural "The Queen at Kingston 1561" in the Entrance Hall

rents and revenues for the maintenance of the School. They were to *"make suitable and beneficial statutes and ordinances in writing concerning and touching the rule government and direction of the Master Undermaster and scholars of the aforesaid school"*.

Thus was forged what one might call the umbilical link between the town and the School. The Bailiffs of Kingston, elected annually, just two in number, were given, subject to the Bishop of Winchester whose interest was unlikely to be very great, what amounted to absolute powers over the School. As local government developed this relationship was retained, right up to 1978 when, as the school became independent, the very last meeting of the Kingston Grammar School Sub-Committee of the Kingston Education Committee, was held.

The Royal Endowments of 1564

To obtain some substantial endowment for the School, the Bailiffs again sought royal help and Letters Patent dated 17th May 1564 listed first the properties and land which had been leased to Richard Taverner in 1547 on a 21 year lease (i.e. the portion of the Chapel endowment not already sold off) and then various other items in the Crown's gift, in and around Kingston. Just a few of the entries give the flavour:

"- the rent of three shillings per annum from a tenement of John Robinson, widower, in Kingston, in "le Markett Place", now or lately in the tenure of George Snelling junior.
- the rent of four shillings annually issuing from the messuage or inn at Kingston called Le Crane in the tenure of James Ware.
- the rent of sixpence per annum from the lands of the late John Westbroke lying in a close at Gadbridge, next to Berefield."

16

All the list *"expressed formerly belonged to the Free Chapel of the Blessed Virgin Mary Magdelene, near Kingston upon Thames in the county of Surrey, now dissolved."*

One might say that this was a fairly painless grant for the Queen to make since what she gave was in sum just part of the endowment which had been confiscated by her predecessors. As a sting in the tail the Letters say that a rent, in respect of the endowments, of £18-9-7d should be paid to the Crown; of the excess, 20 marks or £13-6-8d was to the support of the School and the Master. All told the grant covers, besides the buildings immediately surrounding the Chapel, over 110 acres of land, 27 tenements, four inns, eight gardens and one orchard.

Did the School start its life in the autumn of 1561, a few months after the original Charter from Queen Elizabeth? As so often there is no direct answer but there was a Master in post in 1564, John Laurence, a graduate of St John's College, Cambridge. That we have his name and those of the Headmasters from the foundation up to 1800 is thanks to the authors of a *History and Antiquities of the County of Surrey* which was published in 1804. Manning and Bray copied the details from the School Wardens' account book, lost long since. The full list, from Elizabethan times till now, is set out as Appendix A.

A College for Kingston

John Laurence moved on in 1565, to be succeeded as Headmaster by another Cambridge Master of Arts, Roger Foster. We know no more of him, but quite a lot about his successor, Reverend Stephen Chatfield, MA, who was Master at the School from 1573 to 1584. He combined that post with being Vicar of Kingston (1574-1594) and also Chaplain to the Lord High Admiral, Lord Howard of Effingham. In 1585 a national appeal was launched for a major scholastic institution in Kingston. This was done by means of what was called a Church Brief, an Appeal document issued under royal permission. It was addressed to every diocesan bishop, and onward to every parish, jointly by the Archbishop of Canterbury and the Lord High Admiral.

After pointing out that Her Majesty had lately founded a free Grammar School in Kingston, it went on to say that certain well disposed people wanted to bestow *"large summes of money of their private purses towardes the purchasing of certaine lande near adjoining to the saide towne of the yearly value of two hundred pound above all charges and for the building of certaine fair and convenient roomes meet for the said schoole"*.

For this expected school there would be a Warden, a Master and two Ushers, along with 20 poor scholars *"with meate, drinke, and lodging and their gownes yerely"*. The cost of all this being beyond the means of local donors, the bishops were asked to raise contributions from their clergy. Local parish

17

priests should be encouraged to persuade *"all the inhabitants in every their particular parishes as occasion and opportunitie shalbe offered to give and contribute to the purposed worke aforsayde"*.

Details were given as to how the money raised should be handled, Church wardens sending their local collections to a nominee of the bishop. These were then to send on their gifts to Stephen Chatfield, chaplain to the Lord Admiral, and governour of the said schoole of Kingston and to Nicholas Zouche, gentleman, within five months, at *"the house of Master Walley Stacioner at the great North-doore of Paules who are appointed to receive the generall collection of this contribution"*. The document is dated 4th August 1585 at the Court of Nonsuch.

Unfortunately, the Brief itself is the only document that remains to tell the story. We do not know where the proposed school was to be built, who the local donors would have been, how much was raised nor to what purpose the proceeds were put. They certainly did not go to new school buildings, employment of extra staff, or installation of twenty poor scholars! The only hint comes from what Chatfield's curate John Udall had to tell. He was a fervent Puritan and was associated with William Penney in writing a series of pamphlets entitled the Marprelate Tracts attacking the Episcopal government of the church. One of these made a vicious attack on Chatfield claiming that £260 had been raised for the College of Kingston; but that all of it had been squandered. Given the official nature of the appeal and also that Chatfield remained Vicar of Kingston for another 9 years till 1594, the accusations seem unlikely to be true. Udall himself was sentenced to death in 1590 for attacking the Queen's authority but was pardoned in 1592, dying the same year.

With the failure of this grandiose scheme to turn the School into a college similar to that at Westminister, the story of the School under Elizabeth I comes to an end. But what was school life like for the boys at Queen Elizabeth's Kingston foundation?

School Life in Elizabethan Times

We can build up quite a full picture of what it must have been like to attend school in those days, the school building, the teachers, the curriculum and the school rules. Some of the information is from the records, and some, assembled by RH James, senior History master at the School in the early 1950s, comes from what is known at other Grammar Schools of the time.

First then the buildings. From the foundation, classes were held in the Chapel itself, exactly the same size then as in 1352, a simple oblong whose internal dimensions were 37'9" by 17'3". The churchwardens book for Kingston Parish Church, 1566-1567 shows that the old windows were taken out of the Chapel and installed in the church noting that, *"the old glase .....came from the freskyll sometyme called the chappell"*. No doubt other of the

Hereas the Queenes most excellent Maiestie, hauing heretofore of her gracious and liberall disposition, founded in her highnesse Towne of kingstone vpon Theamis, in the Countie of Surrie, a free Gram= mer Schole, with a stipend of twentie poundes yerely for the Schole= maister is lately giuen to vnderstand of a charitable entent of sundry of good habilitie thereabouts well disposed, to bestowe large summes of money of their priuate Purses, towardes the purchasing of certaine Landes neare adioyning to the sayde Towne, of the yearely value of two hundreth poundes aboue all charges, and towardes the building of certaine other faire and conuenient roumes meete for the said schoole. Whereby might be maintained for euer, a Scholemaster, two vshers, with conuenient Salaries, and twentie poore Schollers with meate, drinke and lodging and their Gownes yerely, together with a warden being a preacher, for the gouernment and ouerseeing of al the rest: which summes neuerthelesse, considering the proportion of the Houses to be builte, and Lande so to be pur= chased, will not (by a greate deale) arise to that which is necessarily to be expended thereon. And for that it were greatly to be lamented, that so bountifull liberalitie already offered, should faile to the ground, and so good a worke be impeached in defect of a conuenient supply yet wanting. It hath pleased her excellent Maiestie of her tender care in setting forth Gods glory by so necessarie a worke, to commit ouer the direction for furnishing vp of such supply, vnto vs the Archbishop of Canterbury, & the Lord Haward of Effingham, Lord high Ad= mirall of England. We therefore according to our bounden dueties, taking care hereof, haue resolued of a conuenient course herein, and for the accomplishment thereof haue thought good earnestly to recommend the cause vnto your L. praying you most instantly, as well to deale effectually with those of your Cathedrall church, and such other of the Cleargie & Lai= tie of your Cittie as you shal thinke good, for a voluntary and free contribution towards so charitable a worke, as also in her Maiesties name to recommend the same, to the like carefull endeuour of three or fower preachers or other discreete ministers in euery Deanry of your Dioces, to the end they may moue and exhort all the rest of the Cleargie within their Dean= ry by them being assembled, not only to giue and contribute to so necessarie a worke, but also earnestly to perswade all the inhabitants in euery their perticuler parishes, as occasion and opportunitie shalbe to them offred, to giue and contribute to the purposed worke aforesayde, as God shall enable them and moue them. Which money so yeelded and collected by the Mi= nister and Churchwardens of euery Parish, with a note vnder their handes of the seuerall summes, may forthwith be payde to such as you shall commit this trust vnto, who are spee= dely to returne the sayd perticuler summes, together with that which shalbe leauyed in the Cathedrall Church and Cittie to your L. that then all the collection made in your Dioces, with the seuerall notes of the whole contribution, may summarily within sixe monethes, af= ter the deliuery of these presentes, or of the copies thereof, be returned & payd ouer at Lon= don to Stephen Chatfield, Chaplein to the lord Admirall, and gouernour of the said schoole of kingston, and to Nicholas Iouche Gentleman, at the house of Maister Walley Statio= ner, at the great North=doore of Paules, who are appointed to receiue the generall collec= tion of this contribution. And so nothing doubting of the good care, furtherance, and fideli= tie both of your L. and the rest to performe the premisses, considering the qualitie of the mat= ter, and from whome it is recommended vnto vs, wee commit you to Gods holy tuition. From the Court at Nonsuch the fowerth of August. 1585.

Your louing frendes.

Iohn Cantuar.

Charles Haward.

The national Appeal of 1585 for funds to build a new school

small buildings attached to the Chapel were used – they were all available. The Chapel became known, certainly in the 19th century, just as "the big schoolroom". So far as we know the only new building was a school house constructed during Stephen Chatfield's time at a cost of £75-16-8¹/₂d. This presumably replaced the house next to the kitchen on the west side of the Chapel in the list of 1547.

Secondly, the teachers. There were only two, the Master and the Usher. The former was almost without exception a graduate of Oxford or Cambridge University no matter whether the School was in good or bad shape. The Master got £20 a year and the Usher £5 plus board and lodging. Clearly the Usher must often have borne the brunt of the teaching. Master Stephen Chatfield combined the role of Master with that of Vicar of Kingston and Chaplain to the Lord High Admiral. If a staff of just two seems small remember that so was the number of pupils. The only recorded occasion before the late 19th century when numbers got up to 100, and when it became necessary to take on extra teaching accommodation was in the mid-18th century. Though we do not have any school rolls for the early days, it seems unlikely that numbers would have exceeded 40-50 and may well have been a lot less. Space was limited, there were only two teachers and the School was for sons of Freemen of the Borough.

Thirdly, the curriculum. Grammar Schools followed what amounted to a National Curriculum and at the heart of it was Latin Grammar. In this connection the compulsory text book (which continued in general use right up to 1867) was *Lily's Grammar*. Henry VIII went so far as to issue a royal proclamation that all schoolmasters and teachers of grammar who wanted to avoid his displeasure would *"teach and learn your scholars this English introduction here insuing and the Latin grammar annexed to the same and none other".* In addition to the Grammar, the master dictated each day a long list of words for the pupils to learn by heart. Once pupils had a good grounding in grammar they started on reading Latin authors (the teaching of Greek in grammar schools was rare). Cicero, Virgil, Terence and Ovid were amongst the most popular but Julius Caesar, Livy, and some of the medieval Christian writers also had a place. Pupils were taught to write Latin compositions. Translations were made from Latin to English, then a few days later translated back into Latin when a comparison was made with the original! The oldest pupils went on to verse composition.

Arithmetic, history and geography had no separate place in the curriculum, scraps of information being picked up no doubt, en route. John Brinsley in his book *The Grammar Schools* published in 1616 wrote:

"You shal have schollers, almost readie to go to Universitie who yet can hardly tell the number of Pages, Sections or other divisions in their bookes, to finde what they should. .... a great and foule want: because without the perfect knowledge of these

numbers schollers cannot help themselves by the Indicies, or Tables of such bookes, as they should use, for turning to anything of a soudaine."

The other subject which did figure largely was instruction in religion and morals. In all grammar schools, the school session began and ended with religious services and Kingston would have been no exception. The original school statutes which the Governors were required to produce, in 1561, have not survived. The earliest extant is from the latter part of the 17th century, in 1671, when George Morley was Bishop of Winchester (1662-1684). Amongst other requirements are these, which may well have been carried through from earlier versions as they are paralleled in Elizabethan Statutes for other schools:

- the children must not neglect the reading of English because they are learning Latin. So every morning the Master is to *"say a short prayer in the English tongue. The assignment of the portion of scripture to be read shall be at his discretion save only that he shall require the books of Proverbs and Ecclesiastes to be read through at least three times in the yeare. And every one of the Schollars shall read in his turn and order".*
- It is laid down as important that pupils shall learn to write a fair hand. If the Master is not capable of teaching this he must employ a scholar *"or some other person who writes a fair hand and he shall diligently and carefully teach the children to write".* There is to be no extra charge for this as it is a part of the Master's Office and duty!

As to the school day, it was a long one indeed. This is what the 17th century statutes require of children at Kingston:

"The children thus admitted shall be fully kept to their learning all the days of the weeks (except Sundays Holy Days and the three Saints Days) from seven of the clock till eleven and from one of the clock in the afternoone until five: unless in the short days of winter when the schoole shall begin and end by that light by which they may well see to read: and that throughout the yeare they shall be dismissed on Thursday at three of the clocke, and shall have their liberty on Saturdayes in the afternoones, according to the customs of other schooles."

Nor was Sunday to be a free day. Led by the Master the pupils were to proceed from the School to the Parish Church to join in morning worship:

"The Master shall require all the children of the towne under his tuition to report timely to the schoole, and thence to attend him orderly (according to their places) and reverently to demean themselves in ye seats appointed for them during ye whole time of ye worship and service of God: and ye Master and Usher shall be near them in a seat or seats to take ye oversight of them that they may carry themselves with exemplary dignity and reverence in ye public congregation ...."

The School statutes do not go into how pupils are to behave, but often in the front of the Latin Grammar of Lily a long instructive piece "De Moribus" was printed which listed precepts about personal hygiene, tidiness, and behaviour, which the pupil was expected to translate, and then to observe. Some schools were less reticent. The Statutes of Wells Grammar School, cited by James, gave minute directions of manners; pupils *were to cut their bread at dinner not gnaw it with their teeth, nor tear it with their nails. When drinking, their mouths were to be empty not full, and they were not to pick their teeth with their knives"!*

Holidays were shorter than in modern schools. Holy Days, that is Rogation Days and Saints' Days, were kept as holidays and the pupils usually received two weeks at Christmas and at Easter. With such a curriculum, long school hours and short holidays, it is hardly surprising that discipline was often a problem. The Elizabethan schoolmaster is always portrayed with a rod and a birch and judging by contemporary reports made good use of both. Brinsley made the point in 1616,

"Now this extreme whipping, all men know what a dislike it breedeth in the children, both of the schools and of learning, as they will think themselves very happy, if the parents will set them to any servile or toiling business so that they may keep from schools. And it also workes in them a secrete hatred of their Masters".

This then was the life of the Elizabethan schoolboy at the Grammar School.

CHAPTER 3

—··◆··—

The School in the Seventeenth Century

—··◆··—

THE VICTORIA COUNTY HISTORY OF SURREY states that from the failure of the scheme for a college at Kingston, in 1585 *"until the eighteenth century we know nothing of the school beyond the names of the masters"*. This is an exaggeration, though hardly a wild one. We have some details of some masters beyond their bare names; we have the School Statutes of 1671, records of the Schoolwardens, and an unbroken series of the School annual accounts from 1674 right through the period and indeed onward to the present day. Together they at least provide some glimpses of the School's life, which seems to have been little affected by the dramas played out on the national stage.

The Masters

First then the Masters. Reverend Stephen Chatfield was followed by Simon Kirkton in 1584, and then Justinian Whyting, MA, of Corpus Christi, Oxford in 1588. During his time there is a passing reference by the Bailiffs, in renewing a lease in 1593, that the cost should not be complained of as they have *"suffered the schoolmaster for twenty years past to have a fair piece of ground near the school, well fenced and set with trees, and other commodious fruit, with decent walks in the same for the benefit and comfort of the schoolmaster worth 40s a year"* (Manning and Bray). Mr Correr, of whom we know no more, was appointed in 1596, and Reverend William Denman BA of Clare, Cambridge in 1599. However in the same year, Richard Hancoke, BA, Gloucester Hall, Oxford, took over until 1609, when William Beeley, MA of both Oxford and Cambridge succeeded him. Another double MA, Ambrose Richmond, followed in 1613. In 1620 Reverend Henry Panton became Master. He was an MA of Queen's, Oxford and his successor in 1622, Thomas Tyroe, was a BA of the same college. Then came Robert French in 1626, BA of Sidney Sussex, Cambridge at the time of his appointment.

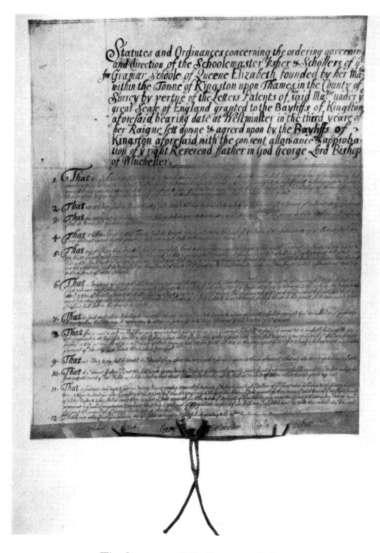

The Statutes and Ordinances of 1671

In 1637 William Burton became Master, the first person of some distinction to hold the post. He was an outstanding scholar of his day and he remained at Kingston for 21 years. Educated at St Paul's School and Queen's College, Oxford he later became a fellow of Gloucester Hall, Oxford where he lectured in Greek. in 1630 he added a BCL to his MA and was awarded a DD in the year he came to Kingston, having left the University for a teaching post as Usher at Sevenoaks after getting his BCL. A brilliant university career was thus interrupted, apparently because of lack of financial means. He published many books, including a History of the Greek Language. Dying of a stroke on 28th December 1657, he was buried in St Clements Dane Church.

William Cooke, an Oxford MA, took over in 1658. According to Manning and Bray, who in 1804 took the details of Headmasters from the Schoolwardens account book, the next master was Dr Hooker in 1663. However, it seems that they missed a Headmaster out. In 1661 Charles II called on the nation for a *"Free and Voluntary present"* to help with the substantial debt incurred in his exile. The list of Kingston donors shows names, occupations, and amount given. There is an entry for Judith Cooke, widow, who subscribed 1/6d. The name of the Master of the Free School, i.e. the Grammar School is given as Mr Bowerman, who subscribed a goodly sum of 10 shillings.[1]

So what happened to Master Cooke? It looks as though he had died, leaving his widow living in the town; alternatively he may have resigned (or been removed) at the time of the Restoration. He was, after all, an appointee of the Cromwellian Commonwealth period. How Manning and Bray came to omit Mr Bowerman from their list must remain a mystery, but they make it clear that their source for Masters' names is far from perfect: *"Christian names are frequently wanting, nor do the dates of their appointments often appear, or whether the new Master comes in on death or resignation"*.

Mr Bowerman's successor, Dr Edward Hooker, seems to have lasted only a few months of the year 1663-4. The Letter Patent of the appointment of his successor Charles Parkhurst, mid-year, speaks of the *"voluntary and free resignation of Dr Edward Hooker"*. It may be that he was a Dissenter who was unwilling to subscribe to the 1662 Act for the Uniformity of Public Prayers passed after the Restoration. That Act required *"every Schoolmaster keeping any Public or private school and every person instructing or teaching any youth in any house or private family as a tutor"* to subscribe to a declaration that he would conform to the Liturgy of the Church of England as it was by law established, etc. Charles Parkhurst was succeeded in 1685 by Thomas Rowell, of St John's, Cambridge and Reverend Robert Comyn, MA of Magdalen, Cambridge, appointed in 1699, saw the century out. A layman was not to be Master again until 1904.

The conclusion has sometimes been drawn from the graduate qualifications held by most of the 17th Century Masters, that the School must have been thriving. This may be so, but the appointment may have been even more attractive if there was but a handful of scholars. The Master received a salary of £20 a year, a house backing on to the School and his private enclosed garden on the other side of the London Road. The old Chapel was a pleasant enough teaching area provided it was not overcrowded; and there was an assistant teacher, the Usher, who could do a lot of the work, leaving the Master time to take private pupils, to engage in scholarly pursuits or take on

---

[1] We are indebted to Tim Everson, Kingston's Local History Officer for the information about Mr Bowerman, which is contained in "A Free and Voluntory Present" by Mr Cliff Webb,.1982.

other outside activities. To be the Master of Queen Elizabeth's Free Grammar School must have carried with it some standing in the community. Finally the School was just eleven miles out of London.

The School Statutes

Secondly there are School Statutes of 1671 previously referred to. Whilst much of their content was probably carried through from the 16th century, the conditions on which boys were taken seem looser than when the School was founded. They are as follows:

"That no children shall be admitted into ye said schoole till having learned to read English they are fit to learn ye rudiments of Grammar.

That for everyone at his admission one shilling shall be given to the Master of ye Schoole and sixpence to the Usher and no more.

That children borne in the Towne shall be taught freely and others that are ye children of the inhabitants of the towne shall pay one shilling a person by the quarter and no more shall be demanded of them."

It will be seen that there was no lower age limit, and no upper one either at this time. Moreover the provisions were not exclusive (i.e. the Statutes did not say that *only* children of the town were to be admitted.) It may well be this loose wording that 60 years later allowed Richard Wooddeson to turn the School into virtually a private academy. There is already in 1708 an intriguing reference to the *"gentlemen boarders"* when the Master complained to the Bailiffs that John Smith's son had *"beat some of the young gentleman boarders at the school"* (Wakeford, p.65). Not that every parishioner was entitled to have his sons taught at the school. In a provision that sounds to be directed against the Dissenters, the Statutes provide that anyone who is unwilling to have his child attend the parish church with the school on Sundays shall not *"have the privilidge of having him taught at the schoole"*.

The Schoolwardens

Thirdly, towards the end of the 17th century, we find references in the minute book of the Borough Court of Assembly, to the role of the Borough's Schoolwardens. They were to supervise the School property, see to repairs, and ensure rents were collected, presenting annual accounts to the Court, which was the assembly of Freemen, and the predecessor of a town council. Cowan (op.cit.) says this:

"Until 1688 they are not named but after that date an almost unbroken list can be compiled. Until 1711 only one was appointed each year, but from then on there were invariably two. The practice was for the Senior Warden to have an assistant who would succeed him the following year, thus every warden served two years, the first as junior warden learning the job, the second as senior, teaching the assistant."

The first extant entry is in 1680 when the Schoolwardens were instructed by the Court of Assembly *"to well and sufficiently amend and repair the rooms of the School at the West end thereof."* The Master, Mr Rowell, was to pay for the repairs, and recover the costs from the rents. If these were insufficient, the Corporation *"would make effectual care for the repayments ..... some other way."*

Entries about the work of the Schoolwardens became quite commonplace in the 18th century, but unfortunately tell nothing of the school life, pupil numbers or curriculum.

The School Accounts

Finally, there is what we can learn from the Annual Accounts, of which the first surviving copy is that for 1674. They have a common form. Year by year, on the left hand are listed, in detail, the rents received. On the right hand are listed the salaries for the Master and the Usher, together with details of the expenses of maintaining the School itself. There is nothing at all about how the School was operating, the number of pupils, curriculum or achievements, but still there are some interesting glimpses. First, the salary remained at £30 (£20 to the Master for himself and £10 to his Usher) throughout the last quarter of the century. Second the rents, which came from ordinary leases (6) and from fee farm and quit rents (46) were, in every year except one, in excess of expenditure. The biggest annual rent in 1675-6 was £5-6-3d for eight acres of land let on Littlefield and Marshfield. Leases made up £15-10-1d and fee farm and quit rents the balance to £42-00-4d. Expenditure that year was £40-15-00d. Through to the end of the century the accounts remain much the same with income varying between £40 and £55, and expenditure a few pounds behind. Finally there are the tantalising items! *"To Boakes the labourer for ditching about the overflow"* (1674) 6/-; *"to Mr Samman for a rope for the bell"* (1675) 2/-; then from 1691 onwards *"to Mr Trippett a years salary for looking after the clock"* 10/-. The works carried out in 1680, and ordered by the Court of Assembly must have been substantial. The School bought 6000 2" nails, 4000 3" nails and 700 6" nails! Another entry, for 1686, is intriguing *"to bread and cheese and boose for the workmen"*. In 1696 Mr Beals was paid 1/6d for *"mending the Gates and the Bridge belonging to the Chappell playing fields."* There is however one entry that comes up again and again, payments to the glazier to repair windows, a clear indication that these buildings were in use as a school, and at just the same risk from stones and balls as any modern school might be. Typical entries just say so much *"to the glazier"* but sometimes they are more explicit for instance in 1675 when the entry was *"To the Glazier for mending the windows of the schoole"*. In the last year of the century, a new Master having taken up office, we read, *"for hedging and ditching the garden 13/-"*. A nice touch this, suggesting that towards the end of Master Rowell's time the Master's pleasant garden across the London Road had not been kept in good order!

What it all adds up to is that if the School was not doing anything spectacular, still at the end of the century it was in business as the town's premier school. "Premier" because during the 17th century the first elementary schools came into being, one supported by a bequest of Elizabeth Brown in 1648 and others by the bequests of two brothers, Thomas and John Tiffin dated 1638 and 1639 respectively. Thomas Tiffin left £60 to be invested in land which would then be let out for rent. The bailiffs were to choose the sons of honest poor men to be taught to write and cast accounts. Browns charity provided funds for clothing 28 poor girls, with a mistress employed to teach them reading and needlework.

CHAPTER 4

—··◆··—

The Wooddeson Era at Kingston
– the Eighteenth Century

—··◆··—

T HE 18TH CENTURY SAW the nadir of the Endowed Grammar Schools in England. Strictly bound by their foundation documents as to what they were to teach, their classical curriculum was increasingly out of touch with the needs of a society moving from an agricultural basis into a merchant venturer and industrial culture. It might still produce some statesmen and classical scholars, but little else. The Grammar Schools decayed. For instance, James (op. cit.) tells us that the minutes of the *"Guild Merchant"* dated 13th February 1765 record of Guildford Grammar School: *"there is not one scholar taught in the said school nor has been nearly a twelve-month past so that the places of Master and Usher are reduced to sinecures ... owing to the intolerable negligence and misbehaviour of the Master."*

At St Saviour's Grammar School, Southwark in 1746 the Governors found that Samuel Willan, the schoolmaster had *"often absented for many days together and very often came into the schools disordered with liquor ... although in former times there had been near one hundred scholars there now are not above ten."*

In 1795 Lord Chief Justice Kenyon scathingly described the grammar schools as *"empty walls without scholars and everything neglected except the receipt of the salaries and emoluments."*

Master Henry Winde (1702-1730)

Here in Kingston in 1702, Reverend Henry Winde succeeded Robert Comyn as Master. He was to remain at Kingston until 1730. Perhaps to remind him of his duties, the Schoolwardens were instructed, in 1703, to have a copy of the School Statutes framed and hung in the schoolroom (i.e. the Chapel). Of Mr Winde's 28 years as Master nothing was known, save what could be gleaned from the annual accounts (he got his salary; year by year the buildings were maintained, the rents collected), until a remarkable document was located in the Hampshire County Records Office, in 1998. This was a lengthy petition from Henry Winde to the Bishop of Winchester in 1725 complaining that the Bailiffs, who were also the School's two Governors, had without reason cut his salary from £30 per annum to £20 in the year 1724. The Bailiffs' argument was that the salary of £30 was made up of £20 for the Master and £10 for the Usher he was supposed to employ. As the Master was doing without an Usher he was only entitled to £20. The Master's counter argument was that the annual accounts said nothing of this but simply recorded year on year a payment of £30 as *"salary to the schoolmaster"* or similar words. Henry was right. He seems to have won the argument for the school accounts for 1725 show him paid £30 plus £10 arrears. But it was a pyrrhic victory and in 1727 under the entry *"Paid Mr Winde his salary"* the amount is entered again as £20! Maybe the Bishop settled the dispute by accepting that the position was unclear for the past, and telling the Bailiffs to pay up for the years 1724 and 1725; but indicating, for the future, that where an Usher was not being employed the Master's salary was only to be £20. Mr Winde left in the Spring of 1730. Though the Petition was about his salary, the document throws a shaft of light on relations between School and town at the time. To the objection that *"this School is of no use or benefit to the town of Kingston"* which he expects to hear, Mr Winde says the Master can hardly be blamed, as he can only teach the children that are sent to him. He goes on:

"I may divide the town of Kingston into two parts, the Gentry and the Tradesmen. The Gentry tho' pretty numerous have not one son fit to come to school amongst them all .... The Tradesmen may again be divided into two parts, the Richer and the Poorer. The first sort only are desirous to have their children instructed in Grammar learning, and they too have only four children amongst them; those that have send them to my school but are well pleased with the pains and care I take with their children. The meaner sort of Tradesmen do not so much as desire their children learn Latin, being employed at their trades or in running upon errands as soon as they are capable of doing anything; and there is a Charity school and other schools where they are taught to read and write, and that is the highest pitch of learning they have in view, or indeed can bestow upon their children tho' they may have been taught gratis."

So it seems there were just four Kingston boys at the School; but the total number of pupils may have been considerably more, since as already noted there was a complaint in 1706 (when Mr Winde was already Master) that a day boy had attacked one of the gentleman boarders.

The Petition also had something to say about the School's Elizabethan endowments which had been set out in detail in Letters Patent from Her Majesty in 1564 (what Henry Winde calls the second charter). If the Bishop of Winchester at that time, and his successors, had been kept in the picture, as they should have been since they were the responsible overseers of the Schools' affairs then *"the lands and tenements mentioned in the Queen's second Charter could never have been alienated and imbezzled as they have been in so shameful a manner. But instead of that they kept the Charters as great secrets amongst themselves, especially the second, which nobody knew of till very lately, no not so as those present Bailiffs themselves."*

Later in the document he goes on to say this of the Bailiffs:

"They have books (which they very much value themselves upon) which show for a hundred years what money they have yearly received of the School rents and how it has been dispursed from time to time. I cannot but say that these books have all along been very well kept; but alas the money that has ever been applied to the School is nothing but the scraps and refuse of the Queens Royal Endowment, being made up chiefly by quit rents and fee-farm rents which are very troublesome in collecting, but the substantial part thereof is lost and gone."

When he wrote this Henry Winde had been Master for 23 years, so should have known his Kingston well. What he seems to be saying is that from the very outset, in the 1560s, the Bailiffs decided to siphon off part of the endowment which belonged to the School to other purposes, private or public, leaving in the School Accounts sufficient rental income to meet the outgoings, but no more. Whether or not this was the case, what is certainly true is that the well kept School Accounts of the later 17th Century make no reference to some of the major endowments, and with the Borough's Bailiffs being the school governors and the Bishop of Winchester clearly not keeping a weather eye open, the possibilities for what one might call *"certain transfers of funds"* were large.

Henry Winde was succeeded in 1730 by Reverend Samuel Heming, MA of Queen's College, Oxford, who only stayed for two years.

Then, in 1732 by some remarkable stroke of good fortune, the governors appointed a man as Master who was to become known as one of the most able teachers of his generation in the country; and what is more he was to stay at Kingston for 40 years. That man was Reverend Richard Wooddeson. Whatever the general state of schools might be it was the case, as always, that a brilliant teacher would attract scholars. And so when Guildford Grammar School was without pupils, just a few miles up the road towards London, the school at Kingston had outgrown the Chapel building and had upward of 100 scholars.

Wooddeson – the Man

Richard Wooddeson was born in 1704, son of the vicar of Findon in Sussex. A chorister at Magdalen College, Oxford as a boy and then as an undergraduate, he took his BA in 1722 and his MA in 1725. From 1725 to 1728 he was the College chaplain and then spent 4 years as an assistant master at a school in Reading, coming to Kingston as Master when he was just 28 years old. He had one son, taught at the school, who became one of its most distinguished old boys (see p. 37). He seems to have made little financial gain from his time at Kingston. When he died in 1774 at Chelsea, just two years after his retirement, he left his widow unprovided for. But he was a great teacher. Gilbert Wakefield, a former pupil (see p. 38) wrote *"on this gentleman I never reflect but with sensations of pleasure and sentiments of respect. He was indeed beloved of all his scholars"* (Memoirs Vol 1,.p. 42). The poet Edward Lovibond (see p. 36) in *Poems on Several Occasions,* 1787, paid this tribute to his schoolmaster of many years before:

> *"There the good teacher held by turns to youth*
> *The blaze of fiction and pure light of truth.*
> *Who less by precept than example fir'd*
> *Glowed as he taught, inspiring and inspired.*
> *Nor think, gay revellers, this awful roof*
> *Echoed no sound but Wisdom's harsh reproof;*
> *The social Board, attendant mirth was there,*
> *The smile unconscious of tomorrows care,*
> *With every tranquil joy of wedded life,*
> *The gracious children and the faithful wife."*

> *(On the converting of the late Mr Wooddesons' House at Kingston*
> *into a Poor-house, and cutting down the great walk of high trees before it)*

Wooddeson – the School

It seems that the Statutes of 1671 were still operative when Wooddeson took over, as in 1722 the master copy of those orders were taken and read over to the then Master, Henry Winde, the suggestion being that he needed reminding of his duties in some respects. These were very loosely worded and did not exclude boys from outside the Borough being pupils. It was only six years on, in 1738 when Wooddeson needed to hire a large house in Norbiton; the mansion house called New Brickhouse is how it was described at the time, though it ended its life in the 1970s as 155-157 London Road. The School was then on two sites and certainly had many boarders, though what was done on which site remained unknown, as does detail of the curriculum. Gilbert Wakefield says that Master *"was very rigid in requiring elegant English from his scholars in construing Greek and Latin authors, almost to a degree of fastidious affectation"* (op. cit.). The only pen picture of school life at that time is in W D Biden's *History of Kingston,* published in 1852, 80 years after Wooddeson's retirement:

"This School obtained considerable celebrity about a hundred years ago, under the able management of Mr Wooddeson who was obliged to hire another house in

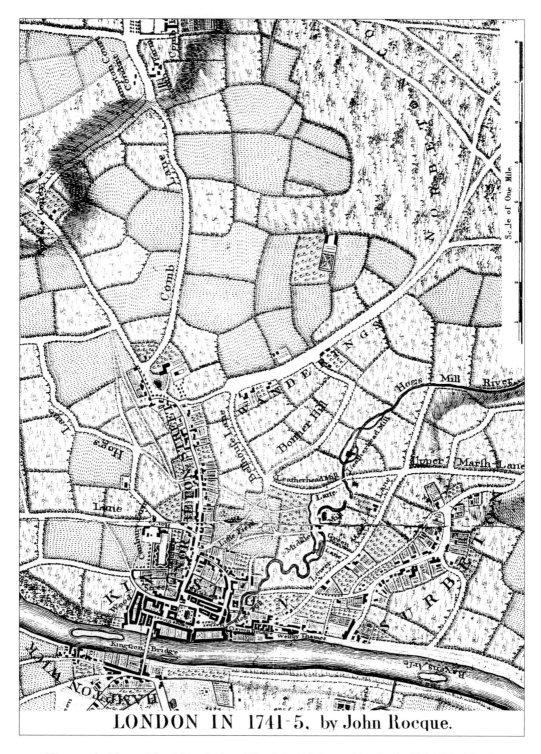

LONDON IN 1741-5, by John Rocque.

Kingston in Master Wooddeson's time (The School is located by the final N of Norbiton)

33

consequence of the large number of scholars placed under his instruction. The scholars under Mr Wooddeson's care varied in number from eighty to one hundred, and consisted of members of aristocratic families alone, who not only claimed none of the privileges of the School as a Free Endowed School, but in the only case in which those privileges were claimed, so maltreated the unfortunate youth whose father had the temerity to seek those advantages, that he was mercifully removed, thus the intentions of the Royal Founder were for a time entirely frustrated."

This picture is echoed in a single sentence of Manning and Bray's *History of Surrey* (1804) which reads: *"The Master has now a Salary of £20 for himself and £10 for an Usher, but no boys belonging to the Town have been sent to the School for a great many years."*

It is interesting that despite the fact that he was running what amounted to a private academy for the sons of the gentry of South West London, Wooddeson continued to receive his Master's salary every year till he retired, and the School buildings on the Chapel site were still repaired as necessary. It may be a combination of two factors that allowed this situation to continue. First, there seem to have been very few people in Kingston who wanted to send their boys to the School. Henry Winde in 1725 only had four. It was not as though the Grammar School was the only school by that time. *"Throughout the 18th and 19th centuries, private academies and dame schools flourished, patronised by the well-off. Poor children, if they were fortunate, also went to school"* (Shaun Butters *The Book of Kingston*, p.135). At the same time, the School cost the Corporation nothing at all. The endowment income nearly always exceeded expenses. This was so right through the Wooddeson era. He paid for the extra accommodation and the extra staff that a school of such a size, up to 100 pupils and largely boarders, must have required. Secondly, Kingston worthies may well have relished having such a distinguished pedagogue at their school. Moreover if over many years there were 80 to 100 pupils, this must have brought useful trade to the town.

Wooddeson's Legacy – His Alumni

In the first 172 years of its life there is no record of anyone of distinction in any walk of life having been educated at the Grammar School. In the next 40 years, those of Wooddeson's Mastership, no less than nine of his boys went on to such fame and fortune that they merited entries in the Dictionary of National Biography.

Edward Gibbon (1737-1794) was certainly the most famous of this group, author of *The Decline and Fall of the Roman Empire*. Unlike Wakefield and Lovibond, he was far from happy in his days at the School. In his autobiography, *Memories of My Life*, he wrote:

"In my ninth year (1746) in a lucid interval of comparative health my father

The most famous of Richard Wooddeson's pupils

adopted the convenience and customary mode of English education; and I was sent to Kingston-upon-Thames to a school of about seventy boys, which was kept by Dr. Wooddeson and his assistants. Want of strength and activity disqualified me for the sports of the play-field, nor have I forgot how often in the year 1746 I was reviled

Edward Gibbons bookplate

Edward Gibbon Esq[r]

and buffeted for the sins of my Tory ancestors. By the common methods of discipline, at the expense of many tears and some blood, I purchased the knowledge of the Latin syntax; and not long since I was possessed of the dirty volumes of Phaedrus and Cornelius Nepos, which I painfully construed and darkly understood. My studies were too frequently interrupted by sickness, and after a real or nominal residence at Kingston School of near two years I was finally recalled (December 1747)."

So perhaps it might be more accurate to say that Edward Gibbon attended the School than that he was educated at it.

Edward Lovibond (1724-1775) was one of Wooddeson's first pupils, and went to his old college, Magdalen, Oxford. In later years his fame as a poet rested largely on the contributions he made to the weekly newspaper the *World* which numbered Lord Chesterfield and Horace Walpole amongst it contributors. His best loved poem, "The Tears of Old May-day" long had a place in English anthologies.

George Keate (1729-1797) was called to the Bar in 1753, but never practised. An intimate friend of Voltaire, he was a poet, naturalist and artist of some distinction, Fellow of the Society of Arts, and also Fellow of the Royal Society.

The Free Grammar School founded by Queen Elizabeth at Norbiton adjoining Kingston, 1795

William Hayley (1745-1820) left Cambridge without taking a degree, but a gentleman of substance, he wrote poems and biographies. Amongst the latter were a *Life of Milton* and a *Life of Cowper*. A friend of William Pitt whom he persuaded to provide a pension for Cowper, he also knew William Blake who provided the illustrations for his "Ballads founded on Anecdotes of Animals."

George Steevens (1736-1800) went on to King's College, Cambridge when he left the School; the main business of his life was the systematic study and notation of Shakespeare's works on which he worked with Dr Johnson. He had the best collection of William Hogarth's engravings in London, and contributed to two books on that artist.

Francis Maseres (1731-1824) was a mathematician, 4th wrangler in the maths tripos at Cambridge in 1752, lawyer and constitutional reformer. Attorney-General of Quebec 1766-69, he was later Deputy Recorder of London and senior judge of the sheriffs court of London. A man of great wealth he left over £30,000, but none of it went to his old college, Clare, because they never asked him to sit for his portrait!

Richard Wooddeson Jnr (1741?-1829) the Master's only son was a leading legal academic of his day. From the School he went to Magdalen College, Oxford. He was to be a Fellow of that College from 1772 till his death over 50 years later. Elected Vinerian Professor in moral philosophy, he held that position for 16 years. His major work was a three volume study *A Systematical View of the*

Laws of England. He had been called to the Bar, and for many years was the University Counsel.

Gilbert Wakefield (1756-1801) was the son of the Vicar of Kingston and went to the School in 1767. A scholar of Jesus College, Cambridge, he graduated as second wrangler and won a Chancellor's Medal, the highest honour then obtainable in Classics. He became a Unitarian and taught for a while at the Dissenting Academy at Warrington. In the 1790s he produced numerous works on the Classics and became deeply involved in politics as a friend of Fox and bitter opponent of William Pitt. In 1798 he published an attack on the whole civil and ecclesiastical system of the day, maintaining the poor and the working classes would lose nothing by French invasion! Not surprisingly he found himself in prison, for two years; he died shortly after his release.

George Hardinge (1743-1816) went on from Kingston to Eton and then Trinity College, Cambridge. Called to the Bar in 1769, he became Solicitor-General to the Queen in 1782 and her Attorney-General in 1794. An MP for some 20 years from 1784 (for the very rotten borough of Old Sarum), he was a painstaking senior judge in Wales from 1787 till his death in 1816. A vice president of the Philanthropic Society, he is said to have collected over £10,000 for charity.

Clearly there were some very bright children at the Grammar School during the Wooddeson era and in the second half of his period as Master the achievements of old boys must have added to the School's attraction for parents looking at any prospectus.

But it was not to last. Richard Wooddeson left in 1772. Numbers seemed to have dropped immediately under his successor, Reverend John Griffiths who, as he only got his Oxford BA in 1768, can hardly have been more than 25 years old when he became Master. Perhaps the Governors had no wish to find another outstanding pedagogue. In 1774, the mansion formerly occupied by the School was bought for £650 by Kingston Parish for conversion into a workhouse, which it remained for over 60 years. The School rapidly returned to obscurity where it was to remain until the middle of the next century.

CHAPTER 5

——··◆··——

Back into the Shadows (1772–1848)

——··◆··——

REVEREND JOHN GRIFFITHS BA, Jesus College, Oxford, was Master from 1772 to 1780. The School contracted back to the Chapel site within two years of his appointment. To be fair, though, Biden (op.cit.) says that although the numbers declined under Griffiths and his successor Reverend Hugh Laurents (1780-1797) of Pembroke, Oxford *"the scholars were for many years none but scions of the aristocracy"*. The accounts show that both these Masters were paid £30 a year, a figure which was to be unaltered till 1842! Private pupils must have been a necessity to attract Oxbridge graduates of any quality, or ambition.

Under the next Master, Reverend Thomas Wilson, of Sidney Sussex, Cambridge, (MA 1792), who held the position for no less than 35 years from 1797 to 1832, a new set of Statutes was promulgated in 1800 which made some important changes. Rule II stated *"that no scholar shall be admitted to the said school under the age of eight years nor remain therein after he is fourteen"* whilst Rule XIV added that *"no scholar shall be admitted into the said school but by the approbation and consent of the said Governors."* There were no other limitations and so the school remained open to all and sundry in Borough and out Borough who could meet the fees, and the approval of the Bailiffs of the day. There was no limitation to sons of the Freemen of Kingston, nor even to inhabitants of the town.

The fees were raised and the curriculum extended. On entry, 5/- was to be paid to the Master and 2/6d to the Usher. Thereafter *"the Parents or Guardians of the Scholars shall pay to the Master 5/-, for each of them by the quarter, and no more shall be demanded of them, except for books, pens, Ink, Slates and Paper which shall be furnished by the Master at reasonable rates"*. English language, English grammar, Writing, Arithmetic and Merchants Accounts *"are equally necessary to be learned as the Latin Grammar."*

By imposing, for the first time, an upper age limit the Governors, in effect, degraded the status of the School. It was exceptional for a boy to go up to University before reaching the age of sixteen. So these new Statutes made it

39

Orders, Statutes, and Ordinances,

CONCERNING THE GOVERNING AND DIRECTION OF THE

MASTER, USHER, & SCHOLARS,

OF THE

Free Grammar School of Queen Elizabeth

FOUNDED BY HER MAJESTY,

Within the Town of KINGSTON-UPON-THAMES, in the County of SURREY.

By Virtue of the Letters Patents of her said Majesty, under THE GREAT SEAL OF ENGLAND, granted to the BAILIFFS of Kingston aforesaid, bearing Date at Westminster, the First Day of March, in the Third Year of Her Reign; set down and agreed upon by the BAILIFFS of Kingston aforesaid, with the Advice of The Right Reverend Father in God BROWNLOW, Bishop of Winchester, the Fifth Day of March, in the Fortieth Year of the Reign of His Majesty King George the Third.

First, That the Master of the said School, who shall be chosen from Time to Time, shall have no Place of Perpetuity therein; but according to his Labour and Diligence shall continue; and if he shall be found negligent, or to have committed any notorious Crime, or to be of infamous Life; then, upon evident Proof made thereof, before the Lord Bishop of Winchester for the Time being, and upon reasonable Warning given him, he shall depart and another shall be chosen in his Place.

II. That no Scholar shall be admitted into the said School, under the Age of eight Years; nor remain therein after he is fourteen.

III. That for every Scholar, at his Admission, five Shillings shall be given to the Master of the School, and two Shillings and Six-pence to the Usher, if there shall be one duly appointed, and no more shall be demanded by either of them.

IV. That the Parents or Guardians of the Scholars, shall pay to the Master five Shillings, for each of them by the Quarter; and no more shall be demanded of them, except for Books, Pens, Ink, Slates, and Paper, which shall be furnished by the Master at reasonable Rates.

V. That the Scholars thus admitted shall be carefully kept to their Learning every Day, except Sundays, Holidays, and the three Fair Days, from eight o'Clock in the Morning till twelve, and from two o'Clock in the Afternoon till five, unless in the short Days of Winter, when the School Time shall begin and end with that Light by which they may well see to read; and saving that they shall be dismissed on Wednesdays and Saturdays at twelve o'Clock, according to the Custom of other Schools.

VI. That the Master shall cause all his Scholars to learn the Church Catechism, and to be ready to answer it, when required by the Minister, in the Public Congregation, that they may be exemplary to others in Submission to every Ordinance of God, and Order of the Church.

VII. That forasmuch as English Grammar, Writing, Arithmetic, and Merchant's Accounts, are equally necessary to be learned as the Latin Grammar, the Master, or some other Person properly qualified for the purpose, to be provided by him, shall diligently and carefully teach the Scholars the English Language Grammatically, Writing, Arithmetic, and Merchant's Accounts; and for this (being part of his Office and Duty,) he shall not exact any further Payment than is above specified.

VIII. That no Liberty of Play shall be granted, at the request of any Person, oftener than once in a Week, and for no longer Time than an Afternoon, and that only when there is no Holiday in that Week.

IX. That at Christmas and Midsummer the Scholars shall break up for one Month, according to the Custom of other Schools.

X. That on Sundays, Holidays, and solemn Days of Divine Worship, appointed by Authority, the Master shall cause all the Scholars under his Tuition to resort timely to the School; and from thence to attend him orderly, according to their Places, to the Church, and reverently to demean themselves in the seats appointed for them, during the whole Time of the Worship and Service of God: and the Master or Usher shall be near them, in a Seat or Seats appointed for them, to take Oversight of the Scholars, that they may carry themselves with exemplary Decency and Reverence in the Public Congregation, and perform their Duty in each part of the public Worship. And that no Parent that refuseth to have his Child thus ordered at the Church, shall have the Privilege of having him taught at the School.

XI. That no Scholar shall be admitted into the said School but by the Approbation and Consent of the said Governors.

XII. That these Orders, Statutes, and Ordinances shall be printed and hung up in the School, and a Copy thereof delivered to every Governor and Master, upon his entering into Office; and to every Scholar on his Admission.

ORDERS, STATUTES, AND ORDINANCES CONCERNING
THE FREE GRAMMAR SCHOOL OF QUEEN ELIZABETH. 1800.
(Reproduction of an old placard.)

The School Statutes of 1800

The Big School Room in 1799 with the Master's dais beneath window. Reproduced from *The Gentleman's Magazine*, 1811

impossible for any boy to go from the School to University without attending some other school in between. This fact, as James (op.cit.) points out, must have been appreciated by the Governors when revising the Statutes. He suggests the real reason was that the Governors, i.e. the Bailiffs, wanted to change the nature of the School so that it would better fit the needs of the town.

"There was very little need for Latin scholars in Kingston but there was a growing need for boys with some form of general education and a knowledge of arithmetic. The Governors could not stop the provision of (Latin) grammar education: the Charter had specifically stated that Grammar must be taught but they were able to make the acquisition of it less important, and to increase the curriculum by adding new subjects." (James, op.cit.)

School hours were from 8 am to noon and 2 to 5 pm, some one hour a day less than before, the afternoon session in winter being limited *"by the light"*. Wednesday and Saturday afternoons were time off. Holidays were a month at Christmas, and at Midsummer.

A glimpse of the School in 1818 is provided in Carlyle's *Endowed Grammar Schools* in which he says of Queen Elizabeth's Free Grammar School at Kingston:

"The present Master is the Reverend Thos. Wilson, whose salary is £30 per annum, with a pretty good house and garden. He is bound by the will of the founder to teach the classics only but it is said he engaged on his appointment to teach reading and writing also. But very few people send their sons, and at present it is stated that not more than 4 or 5 boys attend, so that the school is considered of very little use to the town."

Carlyle goes on to explain that none but the sons of Freemen are admissible, a statement exactly repeated by the Commissioners of Enquiry concerning Charities in 1826. There was in fact no such specific limitation in the Statutes of 1800. The Commission noted that there was, in 1826, no Usher. There were no boarders, and the School consisted of only fourteen scholars in the foundation.

The Commissioners said that the whole of the income of the property comprised in the patents (i.e. of Queen Elizabeth) was applied for the School *"as far back as can be traced"*. They were wrong on this score. The first such item listed, the George Inn, was already in the town accounts of the 16th Century, treated as Corporation property, and the 80 acres of land in Surbiton which were in the 1564 Royal grant nowhere appear in the rentals given by the Commissioners. In fact, now that the full School rental account from 1674 onwards is available it is quite clear that it was in the first 100 years of its existence that the School was despoiled of its endowments to a large extent, as Master Winde indicated in 1725 (p. 30). For the accounts right through from 1674 to 1874 when the Endowed Schools Trust was set up show little variation in the properties from which rents were received. What is more the leases on the 6 or 7 freehold properties were renewed at steadily increasing rents over the two centuries, which seems to indicate reasonable stewardship of what resources there were. For instance, freehold rents brought in £15-10-1d in 1675, £23-17-7d in 1773, rising to £44-2-1d in 1794, £71-00-7d in 1814 and by 1872 to £192-5-1d.

Little is known of Thomas Wilson but during his time at Kingston he held the office of Bailiff no less than 13 times, thus being in the enviable position for more than a third of the time of being both one of the two Governors and Master.

It seems that in 1829 plans for major alterations were approved by the Court of Assembly. In 1831 the Court was informed that when all available monies had been paid out there would remain a debt of £500, some 10 times that of the annual rental income to the School. It was suggested a public appeal should be launched, though whether this happened is not known. At the same meeting *"a letter was produced from Mr Wilson in which he offered to resign the Mastership of the Free Grammar School on the condition of his being allowed the annual income of fifty pounds during his life."* (*Cowan, op.cit.*)

In 1832 Thomas Wilson resigned, whether with or without his £50 per annum pension the records still extant do not show. The Corporation requested the Town Clerk *"to express their appreciation of the reasons by which they believe he has been induced to resign his office."* Had there been something questionable going on, perhaps in connection with the major repairs project?

The next Master was Reverend John Stansbury, BA Magdalen, Oxford who later got an MA, BD and DD. He was to stay until 1849 when he moved on to become Headmaster of Oundle. This was the last appointment to be made by the Bailiffs of the town as Governors, for in 1835 under the Municipal Corporations Act, Kingston like all other boroughs was reorganised with an elected Council, drawn from three wards. These were Town, Ham and Petersham, and Surbiton. The Council was to consist of a Mayor, six Aldermen and 18 Councillors. The governance of the School was passed over to the Municipal Charity Trustees, appointed by the Court of Chancery. The Bishop of Winchester's role remained unchanged.

With the new Master came a new set of Statutes, dated 1832, to replace those of 1800. The upper age limit was raised to fifteen, and the fees substantially increased. The admission fee was now to be two pounds, plus one pound for the Usher, and 15 shillings a quarter was to be paid for each scholar, plus payment for books, etc as before. So a roll of just 30 pupils was now going to bring in about £100 a year, plus the £30 salary, plus a free house and garden, plus whatever could be made on boarders. We know that the new Master, who may well have insisted on revised terms of remuneration before taking the post did, indeed, take in boarders; for the 1841 census records as living at the *"Chapple House"*, apart from the Master, his wife, their five children and four female servants, the following:

John Bailey	12	Pupil
Thomas Phillips	15	Pupil
Charles B Price	14	"
Andrew A Lyley	13	"
James M Layton	13	"
James Bailey	9	"
Thomas C Button	11	"
William Chambers	21	Assistant

So, in 1841, apart from day-boys, there were seven pupils and the Usher who were living in.

The Chapel, which housed the School, 1799. Reproduced from *The Gentleman's Magazine*, 1811

Town Hall and Market Place, by Thomas Rowlandson 1800–1820

44

Kingston Bridge – Old and New by Thomas Rowlandson 1828

1841 also saw another set of Statutes which took advantage of the 1840 Grammar School Act to widen the curriculum further so that it now provided for English Grammar, Writing, Arithmetic, Merchants Accounts, Geography with the use of Globes, Map drawing, Mathematics, Latin and Greek. Fees went up yet again, from 15 shillings to £1-1-0 a quarter and the Master, whilst his salary remained at £30 a year, got a clear £20 extra for his Assistant. In addition he was to receive six tons of coal a year! An entry in the accounts for November 4th 1846 shows that some effort was being made to provide a better education than before. It just says: *"awarded for books and globes £20"*. This must have been a major step forward – £20 was a lot of money to spend on equipment for a small school, the equivalent of well over £2000 at today's prices.

The place of private pupils during much of the School's history remains obscure. They dominated the School in Wooddeson's time but before and after that there is no indication of what proportion of the students they formed. Thus whilst it is reasonable to assume that the seven boarders shown in the 1841 census were private pupils, we do not know how many boys from the town attended. Were they taught together, or separately? What did they pay? The matter was perhaps more important where the foundation scholars still got free education, a principle long since abandoned at Kingston, where everyone had to pay something. An Inspector's Report at Easingwold Grammar School shows what could have happened:

"I found a school along the middle of which was a partition breast high dividing the scholars into two groups. The Master's desk was fixed in an elevated position and

45

dominated both divisions of the school. He explained to me that the free scholars were on one side and the paying scholars on the other. He had erected the partition he said in defence of his own interests, for unless he kept the two classes of pupils – the sheep and the goats, as he called them – habitually apart the more respectable parents would object to pay, and might perhaps remove their children altogether."

(James, op.cit.)

It seems that even at Kingston there was some division, for Brayley in his *Topical History of Surrey* (1852) says that the Master, Reverend John Stansbury, *"is privileged also to take a few private pupils as boarders and day boarders, for whose use there is an upper school room. The foundation school room is the interior of the ancient chapel of St Mary which was repaired a few years ago ....An irregular dwelling house attached to the chapel, forms the Master's residence."* Brayley speaks of the Master having been appointed *"about ten years ago"* so the picture he gives of the School is around 1842.

Finally it is worth noting that if Queen Elizabeth's School at Kingston only just stayed afloat during this period, it was doing a good deal better than some others. James (op. cit.) states that Whitgift Grammar School at Croydon had no pupils from 1820 to 1870, the Mastership becoming a sinecure. By the 1860's Battersea Grammar School was providing only elementary education, whilst as late as 1879 Guildford Grammar School had only twelve free scholars and one other day boy, being taught by a temporary master.

CHAPTER 6

—··◆··—

From the Old to the New,
under William Rigg
(1849–1883)

—··◆··—

W HEN REVEREND WILLIAM RIGG, MA Pembroke College, Cambridge
took over the Mastership in 1849, the School was not that different
from the establishment Queen Elizabeth founded. There was still
only payment from the endowment for two staff, Master and Usher; the
curriculum, though broader, still had a classics bias; the main school was still
the old Chapel; and the number of pupils remained small. Indeed, as
Wooddeson had discovered, the size of the site was itself a limiting factor,
impeding growth, even if there should be an unexpected demand for entry.

By the time William Rigg retired, in 1883, after 34 years in the post, the
situation had been transformed. The Commission on the Endowed Schools
had brought about radical changes in the running of the School, which had
moved out of the Chapel into new buildings on the other side of London
Road, still in use today. Whilst Speech Days are an occasion for hyperbole,
the Mayor's words in 1881 are worth noting:

*"The Mayor said the President of the Council of Education had commented that
middle class education throughout the length and breadth of England was in a state
of absolute chaos. Thank God they had here in the School a living vital institution,
full of good and full of benefits to those who liked to avail themselves of its advantages." (the Surrey Comet, 30th July 1881)*

And of course, the changes all took place under the scrutiny of the local press,
the *Surrey Comet*. Founded in 1854, after a few years attempting a regional
role, the paper settled for being Kingston's journal of record and comment.
The School's activities were well covered. Whereas virtually nothing is known
of the School in the 1840s and 50s, in the 60s the *Comet* sheds a lot of light, as
does the first visit by an HMI. In the 70s the Governors' minutes become

47

The old school building and Headmaster's house c. 1860

available and from 1883 there is the invaluable addition of the School Magazine.

William Rigg as Master

Some unkind words have been written about Mr Rigg, casting him in the role of the last of the unreformed heads, who really was not much interested in anything to do with education! Cowan (op.cit.) says:

"One gathers that Mr Rigg was well established with a good income and was not unduly worried about his duties; these he left to his assistant who was paid £80 a year. He also held a number of outside posts, including that of Chaplain at the local cemetery. He was also reported to be unduly preoccupied with his rose trees. Things staggered on from bad to worse until 1872."

A very different picture emerges from the contemporary records. The *Comet* first reported the School's activities in 1860 when it was stated that the Headmaster had to provide for the annual prizes from his own pocket, as

48

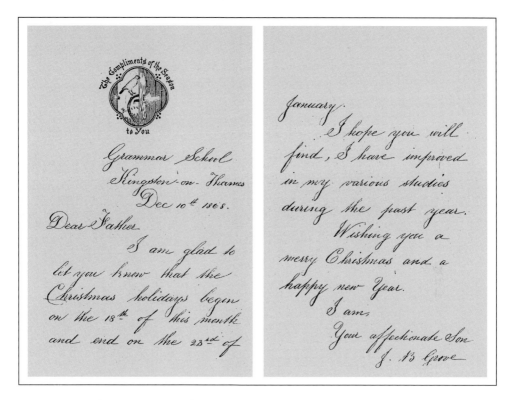

The Compliments of the Season
to You

Grammar School
Kingston-on-Thames
Dec 10th 1868.

Dear Father

    I am glad to let you know that the Christmas holidays begin on the 18th of this month and end on the 23rd of

January. I hope you will find, I have improved in my various studies during the past year. Wishing you a merry Christmas and a happy new Year. I am, Your affectionate Son

J. B Grove

Copperplate letter from a boarder to his father in December 1868

there were no other funds for the purpose. The number of pupils stood at 55 and *"as they all wear college caps the town has something of the appearance of a collegiate town"*. The following year numbers had risen to 59, and regret was expressed that the Trustees could not find the funds to build a new school-room *"which is sorely needed and which is due to Mr Rigg, he having raised the School from 13 boys when he became Headmaster, to its present condition"* (*Comet* 22nd June 1861) It was not till 1871 that the Trustees at last found money for School Prizes.

There is no doubt that for almost all his time at the School, till the new buildings were opened in 1878, Mr Rigg was working under difficult conditions. Around Kingston brand new elementary schools were being opened in purpose built accommodation whilst the Grammar School was still housed in an Elizabethan chapel. Picturesque no doubt but quite unsuited for its purpose in the eyes of contemporaries. Moreover, too near at hand for comfort, a revived Hampton Grammar School was competing for pupils. An advertisement in the *Comet* of 26th December 1868 offers

"under the New Scheme ... a reduced fee of £8 per annum and in the case of two or more boys in the same family, the fee is £8 for one and £6 for each of the others. A

sound religious, classical and mathematical education is guaranteed and boys are prepared for Eton, Harrow and for the universities as well as for commercial pursuits ...."

In something of a cri de coeur, in 1870, the Head expressed his concerns in a long letter to the *Comet*. Inter alia, he said:

1. Not one of the Town Council had been to visit the School in the last 20 years.
2. As the Head he has just £60 a year and has to pay all except the under master from the payments made by the boys. He considers this a disgrace, and doubts if there is another school in England in such a situation.
3. It is impossible to preserve such order in school as he might wish *"when you had to teach four classes or more in a room far too small for them."*
4. There must be something going right for the School, despite all the problems, for he had raised the numbers to 70 on the books (there had been 80), *"but I do not encourage more as there is no room for them at present."*

(Comet, 22nd October 1870)

Another letter, to the Trustees, dated 24th October 1872 seems to illustrate the continuing problems Mr Rigg, by then a very senior Master of 23 year standing, had to cope with:

"I beg to report that the cesspools have not yet been cleaned and they need it very much – they must be done for the protection of myself and family as well as for the boys (57 in number), so if I do not receive orders from you I must have them done and pay for them, waiting until you can afford to pay me. The roof of the whole premises wants looking into. Rain has come in the last few days and the East End and North windows are in such a dilapidated state that something must be done before the winter as no master can sit at the East end."

And that was not all. He was not receiving the money to pay the Second Master (Usher) on time and so was having to advance this from his own income which he could ill afford to do. It certainly does not seem to have been a bed of roses, and whatever his weaknesses it was quite an achievement to bring the School back to something like its original purpose. From 13 scholars all told (of whom half a dozen were boarders) to a regular school roll of 50 plus, touching 70 and more in the best years; nearly all of whom were foundation scholars, was quite a transformation. Perhaps Mr Rigg deserved some time off in his garden!

The Life of the School – the Inspection

The first ever inspection of the School took place in 1865. It happened this way. In 1864, the Government, disturbed at the state of secondary education, appointed The Schools Enquiry Commission to enquire into the education being given in the ancient Grammar Schools. The Commission was *"to Report what measures are required for the Improvement of such Education having special regard to all endowments applicable, or which can rightly be made applicable thereto."* Parallel studies were made of the major Public Schools and of the Elementary Schools. Four assistant commissioners were appointed to visit the Grammar Schools, and it was Mr D R Fearon who came to Kingston.

However, before being inspected a school had to fill in a questionnaire and some of the details make interesting reading. At Queen Elizabeth's Grammar School the knowledge necessary on admission was *"read words of one syllable, writing"*. All 52 boys were said to be learning arithmetic, history, geography, reading and writing and had religious instruction. Latin was being studied by 40 (Greek by only 4), English composition by 40, English grammar and English composition by 12, whilst 10 took French, 10 Drawing and 4 Bookkeeping. There were daily prayers for the whole school and it was still the case that the whole school attended Divine Service at the Parish church on Sundays. Only the Headmaster could cane boys, and did so in public; monitors could either report offending pupils or *"exclude them from the playground"*. Against the item *"Use of Library"* is the sad entry *"None"*.

Mr Fearon was far from happy with what he found on his visit and said so in his Report. Two of the four staff, the writing master and the part time French and Drawing master were not efficient teachers. *"Inferior to any trained national schoolmaster"* was his comment on the writing master. As to discipline, whilst the boys appeared healthy and respectable in manners and dress they were *"not in a good state of discipline. There was much noise and disorder during schooltime in the schoolroom and there was an evident want of quiet method and system in the routine."*

As to the pupils' attainments, Mr Fearon found these very patchy but on the whole felt the results of his examination could not be regarded as satisfactory. He put down the deficiencies to a variety of factors. One was the low entrance requirements, *"their reading at entrance often being very bad, scarcely attaining to the mastery of words of one syllable in a most elementary book, and the writing being frequently nil"*; poor teaching in some subjects, changes of staff, and the fact that boys often came to the school for only a short time, were others. This last comment, expressed as *"boys often come to school old and ill-prepared (to 'finish' as they call it)"*, suggests that townspeople really liked to say their sons attended the Grammar School as a mark of social status rather than for any educational benefit. In fact only three boys had gone on to university, all of them private boarders (of whom there were six at the time living in the Headmaster's house) in 6 years. No foundation scholar was at university.

Of the school premises the Inspector was scathing. The schoolroom was singularly ill-adapted for educational purposes. It needed cleaning, painting, furnishing with desks, maps and good apparatus all of which he found to be *"very deficient"*. In any case it was too small even for the present number of boys (52) and had only one very indifferent classroom attached to it which was equally ill-furnished. The yard playground and offices were also *"very bad"*. As for the Headmaster's house, it was, he said, very old-fashioned, incommodious, and unsuited for the purpose of a boarding house, with low, ill-ventilated rooms. *"In short not at all adequate to the purpose."* In summary, Mr Fearon said:

The whole of the buildings are, in fact, most unsatisfactory. They would not be tolerated as buildings for a National, or Wesleyan, or British school in receipt of Government grants either in respect of their size, shape, furniture or apparatus. They appear to be hardly worth repairing or enlarging."

The conclusion he arrived at was that a new school should be built upon the site of the school garden on the opposite side of the road, utilising some of the funds of various small educational charities in the town, an idea previously put forward in 1861 by the Charity Commissioners, but ignored by the Trustees of the School.

Mr Fearon also wanted the curriculum revamped, so as to make it *"more comformable to what the country now requires for a lower middle class education."* Latin should only be commenced towards the end of a boy's foundation career. English and French, better taught, should have a more prominent place, drawing taught scientifically, music introduced, and lectures on scientific subjects given.

The School Curriculum

At the same meeting of the Trustees when Mr Rigg complained about the state of the cesspools, he submitted a copy of the school's weekly curriculum. This was at the Trustees' request, who presumably wanted to be assured that the Inspector's comments on this aspect of school life had been implemented. The Head produced, on a single side of notepaper, a summary. This was slipped in with the minutes by the Clerk, and so survives to this day. It is reproduced in its entirety below:

The School Week 1872 – Monday to Saturday

9.30-9.50	*Bible reading and prayer. Every day. All classes*
9.50-10.15	*Writing and looking over exercises. Every day. All classes*
10.15-10.35	*Say repetition learned at home everyday (sic) the same*
	viz. 1st class *one week English history, 2nd Scripture history*
	3rd Geography and 4th English Grammar
	2nd class, English history, Scripture history and Geography
	alternately
	3rd class, " " "
10.35-11.05	*Every day Repn. learned at home.*
	1st class, Horace and Primer – alternately, English Grammar

	2nd class, *Primer – alternately, English Grammar*
	3rd class, *Primer – alternately, English history*
11.05-12.15	1st and 2nd classes *Latin construing or English parsing*
	3rd class *Sums*
12.15-12.30	*Same 4 day Greek and youngest boys read. Wednesdays and Saturdays all do tables.*

On Mondays and Thursdays French from 9.50 to 11.20 in two classes, the boys leaving their other lessons for French.

Afternoons	*NB Wednesday afternoon off*
2.00-2.30	1st class *Mon/Tue Latin verbs and Primer*
	Thurs. Kings of England and geography
	Fri. ,, ,,
2.30-3.45	*Sums*
3.45-4.30	*Mon. History of Greece, Rome and England*
	Tues. 3.30 English composition or dictation
	4.00 Catechism and Religious knowledge
	Thurs. Show map drawn at home, read a scientific book and lectures from diagrams on wall maps
	Fri. Read poetry etc.

On Monday afternoons a drawing class from 2 to 4.

It is difficult to draw conclusions from the bare bones of a timetable but three things seem to emerge. First the whole school aged 8 to 15 were being taught in just three classes. Second, the picture given is one of a pretty dusty curriculum, though no doubt it was typical of the grammar schools of the time. And third, the radical changes advocated by the Inspector look to have been implemented in a half-hearted fashion. Mr Fearon had said that Latin should be deferred till "*towards the end of a Boy's foundation career*". Seven years later the Latin Primer still figured in the youngest class. French, he had said, should have a more prominent place. Seven years on it was still an "*extra*". Music should be introduced. Seven years later it was still not on the timetable, even as an "*extra*". As to scientific subjects, there seems to have been the merest nod in this direction when for the last 45 minutes of Thursday afternoon the timetable indicates "*Show map drawn at home, read a scientific book and lectures from diagrams or wall maps*". William Rigg seems to have remained a convinced traditionalist on what should be taught and how!

The Endowed Schools Trust

The Schools Enquiry Commission Report was published in 1868 and included the results of the inspection of the School. Whilst Mr Fearon could make recommendations, he had no power to impose solutions. And whilst the Charity Commissioners had already indicated their willingness to consider plans for the improvement of the School, those plans had to be put forward by the Trustees of the Public Charities of the town, the same gentlemen who persistently refused even to pay for the annual scholars' prizes!

They were 15 in all, a mix of clergy, tradespeople and "gentlemen". Their remit covered all the local charities, not just the School, and whilst the idea of appropriating Tiffin's money and that of other smaller charities for the benefit of a new Grammar School might appeal to some trustees it did not do so to others. The debate raged for over three years in the columns of the *Comet*. The crux of the issue was set out in a Leader in the *Comet* on 9th January 1869 which concluded:

"We wish to see the Grammar School carried on in a building more suited to the purpose than is that wretched apology for a school where it is now held but we would say to the trustees of that charity, do not appropriate £900 for the benefit of those who can afford to pay all the expenses of an education for their children while there is plenty, far too much room, for its application in carrying out the wishes of the deceased Tiffin."

At a subsequent public meeting Mr Rigg said that if the Tiffin Charity could be transferred to the Grammar School, enabling a new school building to be erected, 4 or 5 poor boys would be taken into the Grammar School. There was overwhelming opposition. Some 1250 boys, Mr Drewett said, had been educated in the last five years at the expense of the Tiffin Charity. The meeting decided a memorial should be prepared and sent to the Charity Commissioners begging them not to part with any funds towards the Grammar School, but that the said funds be kept for purposes agreeable to Tiffin's will (*Comet* 2nd February 1869).

It was not until March 1872 that a compromise was worked out which satisfied all the interested parties. It was to build three new schools, not one! The Grammar School should be rebuilt and continue, for the Upper Middle Classes of Kingston. A second school, Tiffin Boys', was to be established immediately as a Lower Middle Class school. A third school, Tiffin Girls', of the same character should be established as soon as possible to provide a *"superior education for Girls."* So everybody won, and all the different charitable funds could properly be devoted to the three good causes. All three schools were of course to become major institutions of secondary education in the years ahead. And one might indeed say that the very existence of the Tiffin Schools stemmed from that Inspection of the Grammar School which launched the education debate in Kingston in 1869.

The Kingston Endowed Schools Trust – the Scheme

The Endowed Schools Commission produced a detailed Scheme to implement the proposals. Out went the Bishop of Winchester and the municipal Charity Trustees and in came a body of 14 Governors, the High Steward of Kingston, 4 nominees from Kingston Council, 2 from Surbiton

Improvements Commissioners, 1 from the New Malden Local Board, 4 from the Trustees of the Municipal Charities and 2 to be co-opted. Nominated Governors served for 5 years only. The document set out how the schools were to be run. For the new Queen Elizabeth's Grammar School the Trustees were to choose from land under their management:

"a convenient and suitable site with sufficient playground and shall erect or otherwise complete thereon a School building with proper classrooms capable of accommodating at least 100 scholars with or without residence for the Headmaster. For this purpose they shall be at liberty to expend the capital funds of the Trust to the extent of £3,000 without taking into account the value of the site."

(Scheme – Section 30)

The Governors were to appoint the Head, who was to receive;

- a salary of £100 a year
- a free house or allowance in lieu
- an annual allowance, from the Governors, of not less than £2 and not more than £4 for each boy in the school (all boys to pay a tuition fee of not less than £6 nor more than £12 per year. These fees to go to the Governors)

The Head could have boarders, not exceeding 12, paying a maximum of £45 per year each for board and lodging.

No boy was to enter the School under 8 and there was to be an examination, graduated according to age, but never falling below the standard of *"Read easy narrative, small text handwriting, the first two rules of arithmetic, and the outlines of the geography of England."* This was a marked improvement on the previous provision. Children of residents in the Parish of Kingston were to be given preference. The Governors were given power to raise the minimum standard from time to time if this seemed advantageous to the School.

Having got in, what was the curriculum that the boys followed? The Scheme lays this down.

"The subjects of secular instruction shall be as follows:
>   *Reading and Writing*
>   *Arithmetic and Mathematics*
>   *Geography and History*
>   *English Grammar, Composition and Literature*
>   *Latin and at least one Foreign European Language*
>   *One or more branches of Natural Science*
>   *Political Economy*
>   *Drawing*
>   *Vocal Music."*

Greek was an extra, to be paid for! There was to be an annual examination, boys were not to stay on after their 17th birthday and £50 a year was to be set aside for Exhibitions carrying total exemption from fees and *"to be assigned on the ground of merit, in the first instance, to boys who are being educated at Tiffin Boys' School."* They are not to be thrown open to general competition *"until the Headmaster of the Grammar School has reported that there are not enough boys from Tiffin Boys' School who on examination prove worthy to take them"*. This put Tiffin School properly in its place, so far as Kingston in the 1870s was concerned. The top education was to be at the Grammar School.

Funding the Scheme – the Endowment

As mentioned the Scheme provided for the amalgamation of all the Charities in the town which were in any way connected with education; and there is a full statement of the property and income, including of course the Grammar Schools. In the published scheme the incomes ranged from £222-12-6d a year (the Grammar School) and £199-18-7d (Tiffin's Charity) through £106 (Henry Smith's Charity) down to £6 (John Hartop's Charity) and a mere £5 (King Charles's Charity). All told no less than eleven charities were brought together and their collective income was £725-8-2d a year. But the really important innovation was that some of the capital could be used to build the new schools, as needed. As to the income from the now established Trust Fund it was to be divided 10/24 to the Grammar School and 7/24 to each of the new Tiffin schools. Up to £4000 of capital could be spent on the buildings for each Tiffin School as well as the £3000 for the Grammar School and they were to be designed to take 150 pupils each. The Trust continued in existence for over 100 years until 1978 when it was dissolved and the remaining assets divided between the Grammar School and Tiffin Boys' under a formal Charity Commissioners' scheme (Tiffin Girls' had opted out in 1940).

The New School – William Rigg's Last Years

The new order took effect in 1874 but the School was still based in the Chapel. Numbers were good, quality was not, as the Head pointed out on prize day, 19th June 1875: *"There are a great many more boys this year than there were last, upwards of 50 new boys having entered during the year and many of them since Christmas: and these, I am sorry to say were not up to the mark."* *(Comet, 25th June)*

The previous year he had bemoaned the fact that the whole of the top form had left during the year for clerkships except one, who had gone into his father's business. As for the new school building, Mr Rigg was preparing everyone at the 1876 prizegiving for disappointment. If the buildings were not so commodious as anticipated he trusted it would be attributed not to a want of will on their part, but to a want of power. The drawings as originally designed were excellent drawings but they proved too expensive. None the

The whole School, 1875, on the School Meadow with Chapel and Headmaster's house in the background

Kingston Gr. School,
Mich^mas 1876.

The Master Mudie's a/c.

	s	d
Collier 3/6. Ellis 2/6 —	6	0
Outline atlas 6^d arith^c & Primer 10^d -	1	4
3 copy bks 1/. Table bks. pens &c. 1/2 -	2	2
	9	6

Quarterage to Xmas 2 .. 2 . 0

2 .. 11 .. 6

Rec^d ... 31/7/6

"Master Mudie's account for Michaelmas term in 1876 including text books, exercise books and fees"

less, the new buildings were a great improvement on the Chapel schoolroom and the move across the London Road took place in January 1878. Numbers collapsed, down to 27 and although by 1881 they had recovered to 52 it was becoming clear that the new buildings alone would not be the salvation of the School. The Head was nearly sixty, and Tiffin Boys' School had opened in 1880 under a very lively head, Mr C J Grist. Advertisements in the *Surrey Comet* in May that year showed what the competition now was. The Grammar School wanted £3/10- termly (plus application fee of 2/6 and entrance fee of 10/6) whilst the sum Tiffin Boys' wanted was just £1-0-0 a term. The curricula were almost identical. By the end of the second term in 1880, numbers at Tiffin were 111 and Mr Grist expected to be full by the end of that year (i.e. 150 pupils). The writing was on the wall for Mr Rigg. A new impetus was needed. He retired in 1883 at the age of 61. He certainly had mixed fortunes but he had battled on and kept the Grammar School going through a very difficult time, especially in his first 20 years in post. When he died in 1892 an "Old Boy" wrote in the School Magazine:

"Those who had the advantage of being under the Reverend W Rigg when he was in his prime will ever have a kind recollection of him. Stern as a disciplinarian and exacting in the work that had to be prepared, he was yet beloved by those of his pupils who knew him thoroughly, for when at football or at cricket, taking part in the bonfire and firework celebrations on Guy Fawkes Day, or personally conducting an expedition to Box Hill, he was a big boy among boys. There are yet some left who can look back upon happy days, in the old school, feel thankful for the example of manliness their Master ever put before them, and will be truly sorry to hear that he has passed away."

And what of the old buildings, Lovekyn's Chapel and the adjoining Headmaster's house? The house was pulled down, leaving the west end of the Chapel ruinous since the house actually abutted it. The Chapel itself became derelict, windows boarded up, and the south wall shored up by timbers. It did not look as though it had any future.

CHAPTER 7

—··◆··—

The False Dawn
(1883–1912)

—··◆··—

A New Head – a New Start

REVEREND W ELLIOT INCHBALD arrived to take over as Head in September 1883, having been head of the Surrey County School at Cranleigh for some years. He was an MA of Clare College, Cambridge where he had been a Classical Scholar, and was to stay until 1903. One of his first actions was to establish a School Magazine, the *Annual Register*, later to become the *Kingstonian*. This gave quite a detailed account of the School's academic, sporting and social activities through each year so it becomes possible to follow the way school life developed. The other main sources of information are the Governors' minute books, and the *Surrey Comet*.

In William Rigg's last year, 1882-1883, numbers had plummeted down to a mere 23. With the new Head the trend was immediately and dramatically reversed. Within 2 years there were 41 boys at the School, and this doubled to 82 in the year 1885-6, to 104 the following year and to 124 in 1887-8. It was this remarkable increase in student numbers, over 400% in five years, that helped to save the Chapel from demolition. For the new buildings were only designed for 100 pupils and already within a couple of years the Head could see they would be inadequate.

The Restoration of the Chapel

The Surrey Archaeological Society wanted to save the Chapel; the Head wanted to use it; townsfolk said it would be a shame to pull it down. But who was going to pay the bill? The Chairman of the Governors, Mr T Guilford, decided to do some networking.

"He offered to give £50 if five other gentlemen would do the same. He applied to five other gentlemen and the first four responded immediately and promised £50

Reverend W Elliot Inchbald,
Headmaster 1883–1904

*each towards the object in view. He failed only in once instance, but he had no
doubt he should get the sixth gentleman before long and that the work would be
done."*

Speech Day, July 1885

The total bill for restoration came to £658, raised without a public appeal.
The Corporation came in with £60 in return for the School setting back the
boundary wall so as to widen London Road and School Alley (which now
became Queen Elizabeth Road).

The "Old School" was reopened on 4th August 1886, the small classroom
having been converted into a science laboratory of sorts, and the main
Schoolroom coming into use for the Upper School. The building was to
remain in use for over 100 years more, becoming a Gymnasium in 1904, then
the home of the Preparatory Form, after a proper gym was built in 1936; and
finally from 1980 to 1992 the Woodwork Centre. At that point in time it was
further restored, for school and community use (see p. 146).

The only other building of any significance in the years up to the First
World War was a new Chemistry Laboratory to the left of the School
entrance, at a cost of £800. This was opened in 1897.

The old building, the Lovekyn Chapel in disrepair (1882) after the school moved out in 1878

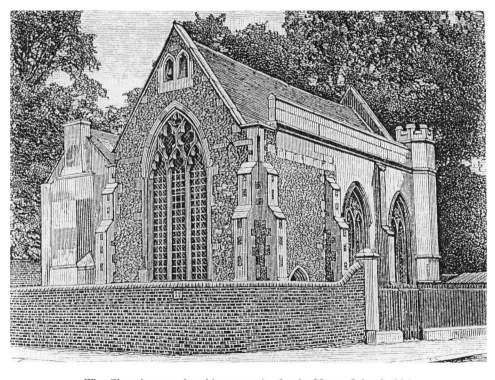

The Chapel restored and in use again, for the Upper School 1886

A Better Education than Before

Ten years after Mr Inchbald's arrival the educational picture had been transformed. In place of a Headmaster with two full time and two part time staff,
there were now seven full time and three part time staff to support the Head.
Four candidates successfully sat the Oxford Senior Local Examinations and
seven the Junior ones. A sixth form had been started in September 1886 whilst
in 1887 a Modern Form had been introduced intended *"for boys who wish to
follow a mercantile career or to apply for a clerkship in some office (at 15). The
Modern Form ranks as the lowest form of the Upper School."* (*Annual Register.*) In
January 1892 a circular was sent out explaining the advantage of shorthand to
boys who were preparing for the mercantile life. So many favourable
responses were received that a class was set up consisting of nearly forty boys.

More Sports than Before

With the rapid growth of the School there were many more opportunities for
sporting activities. Cricket and football were already being played when the
new Head arrived in 1883, though there are no details available. In came
swimming, athletics, cross-country running, and most notably hockey. From
the *Annual Register*: *"This game was introduced into the playground for the first
time last October (1890) and has been carried out with much zeal ... the chief difficulty is to make the whole team act in concert; each member of it is apt to think that
the success of his side depends upon himself alone."*

The full story of the School's sporting achievements in the period up to the
First World War is the subject of Chapter 13.

The School Community

There were big changes elsewhere in the life of the School, the most notice-
able being the introduction of the Prefect system in 1886. The *Register* says
the Prefects are to be appointed by the Headmaster and are to be distinguished from the other boys by having the School monogram, worn on the
cap, of gilt braid; such prefects caps were still being worn in the 1950s. The
duties were:

1. To assist the Masters in maintaining discipline, the observance of the
   School rules especially in the playground.
2. To constitute together with certain of the Masters, a Games Committee
   who shall arrange School matches at Cricket and Football, and exercise
   control over other playground sports.
3. To stop all bullying if any should occur; and generally to protect the weak
   against the strong.
4. To do all in their power to keep a high tone in the School, both by example
   and authority.

An insight into School discipline at this time comes in a report to the

Governors dated 19th June 1886 in which the Head explains why he has expelled a boy for theft.

"He had made a small purchase with a token resembling a sovereign and received 19 shillings in change. The fraud was discovered, and the boy pursued, caught, and handed over to his father who, I understand, punished him severely as he deserved ... Under these circumstances it seemed his influence in the School could not be otherwise than most dangerous. I called upon the boy's father who agreed with me that the gravity of the offences above described (there had also been the theft of a plane from the carpentry room) admitted to no alternative to the instant dismissal of the boy from this School. He has since been sent away from the town altogether. Sincerely regretting that this unfortunate affair should have occurred ...."

If we know little about discipline, we know from the *Register*, a lot about school activities, and not just sports. In 1886 a Literary, Scientific and Debating Society was founded, which met weekly in the two winter terms. In October 1897 this body was re-named the Gibbon Debating Society in memory of that illustrious *"Old Boy Edward Gibbon the Historian."* The average attendance was 15 and the weekly programme alternated between Papers presented by members (or *"Readings and Recitations"*), and formal debates. The subjects during that school year were:

> That the pursuit of wealth is pernicious to the human race.
> That modern civilisation is a failure.
> That man is not master of his destiny.
> That England's foreign policy is far too selfish
> and That Shylock is not so bad as he is painted.

The Gibbon Society has been in almost continuous existence ever since 1897, though it must be many years since its members gave an Entertainment to the whole School of the kind that took place on 15th March 1898. This included Mr R Lockett, an Old Boy, singing "The Deathless Army" and "The Toilers", and a pupil rendering "Star of my Soul" and "Loves Old Sweet Song".

Another feature was the establishment of a School Library in 1891. It was very modest at the outset. *"Some of the boys profess to have read all the books which is very creditable to them as there are 150 volumes,"* (*Register* 1891). In 1893 it was decided that a sum of money, not less than five guineas a year (i.e. £5.25p) should be set aside from the Literary and Athletic Fund for the purchase of new books. Every boy in the school had free access to the Library at stated times. Senior boys were appointed as librarians. By 1898 the Library boasted 400 books and was still expanding. The total was 470 by the turn of the century!

Drill, with or without arms, was a regular feature of School life and led up the Annual Drill Competition, of which the 1894 event was typical:

"It consisted, as usual, of physical exercises with and without arms horizontal and parallel bars, ropes, dumb-bells and single stick. Considering that the majority of the squad had barely been members for a term their general efficiency and smartness reflect great credit on their instructor, Sergeant-Major Brain." (The Register)

All told the picture at Queen Elizabeth's School ten years or so into Mr Inchbald's time as Headmaster was a pretty rosy one. Numbers had settled at a reasonable level, varying between 118 and 136 during the years from 1888-9 to 1894-5. The School was doing well. Yet within the next decade all this was to turn to ashes. What went wrong?

Decline and Fall

Quite suddenly the School faced a drop in numbers almost as dramatic as the increase experienced in the first few years of the Head's time. From 122 in 1895-6 the number of pupils fell to 76 in 1900-01, a drop of over one third in just five years. What had happened? First, the competition for pupils had intensified. Tiffin, now established some 15 years, had an excellent reputation and was much less costly. In 1897 fees were £3 a term compared with £5 a term at the Grammar School. Hampton Grammar was still in the field and a very distinguished school, King's College School, had just moved into Wimbledon from London. All of them had good buildings whereas a Board of Education Inspector was to say of Queen Elizabeth's in 1903 that there was nothing in the buildings which *"would prove attractive to a parent coming to look at the School and much which would be quite the reverse of attractive."* There was still a social cachet locally in sending one's son to the Grammar School but to a large extent boys left the school very young either to go into commerce or to move to another school. In 1902 eleven out of 21 leavers were under 15 years of age. There was no significant sixth form. Boys were just not going on to University direct. So the parent who wanted a school right up to University entrance level was not likely to send a son to the Grammar School. Given all these factors it is not difficult to see why the new entrants might steadily decline. And, of course once the decline set in, this of itself would suggest a "failing" school, and reinforce parental doubts. Fewer pupils meant fewer staff, probably with fewer curriculum options, and reduced school activities.

By April 1903 the School's debts, which had accumulated as a direct result of the serious drop in the School Roll, led the Governors to consider drastic action:

"Mr Wilkins then moved that having regard to the financial position of the Queen Elizabeths School and the increasing annual deficit in its accounts the time has now arrived when it has become necessary – unless the Governors are able to obtain from the County Council some sufficient assurance of financial aid now and in the future – to close the School and that steps be taken at an early date accordingly."

(Governors Minutes)

The Resolution was passed by 9 votes to 2. It may really have been aimed at the County Council who, although the Grammar School had become recognised as the First Grade School for Kingston by the Board of Education in 1897, still refused to make a substantial annual grant of the kind awarded to Tiffin School. In the event a Board of Education Inspection took place at the beginning of June, and its result overshadowed the concerns expressed by the Governors in April.

The Board of Education Inspection June 1903

On recognition as a First Grade school the Grammar School accepted supervision within the state sector, and this would remain the case right up to 1977, when it again became an independent school. The Board of Education Inspectors spent two days in the School and produced a report of the kind which every Head fears the OFSTED team may come up with these days! There were good points. The Headmaster had done good service, and to a large extent the fall in numbers over recent years was due to external factors; the staff were well qualified; and boys well cared for; discipline was excellent; and there was a full social and sports life.

For the rest they found that *"the buildings, if judged by the modern standard are seriously wanting."* And this only 25 years after they were put up. In the school rooms *"the want of tidiness and care is very marked and the whole has a homeless and unattractive appearance. The addition of an Art Room and a Gymnasium is desirable and a proper changing room is much needed ...."* The Inspectors felt it was their duty to put the following on record:

"In view of the very serious question concerning the future of the School now awaiting decision, excellent though his work had been in the past it might reasonably be expected that a younger Headmaster, fully cognisant of new developments of teaching might raise the School both in name and position."

Of the School as a whole their comments were damning:

"The School does not seem to have attained any successes in University or other examinations in respect of boys either actually in the School or coming directly from it, and in this matter it is undoubtedly below the standard of the ordinary Grammar Schools .... The recent diminution of numbers shows that the Grammar School is not good enough to stand against any competition, but points to the need for its improvement rather than its superfluousness. The School is not inefficient but it is entirely without distinction .... If the present School attracts 70 boys then an improved school ought to have quite double the number."

The final sentence of the Report reads, *"Unless the buildings and finances of the School can be improved as suggested it is not clear that the continuance of the School can be justified."*

In summary the Inspectors said that if the School was to have a future, it needed better buildings, a new Head, and sounder finances which in the main would come from developing into a proper Grammar School taking boys right up to University entrance.

All Change at the School

The Governors received the Inspectors' Report on 17th December 1903, concluded it was an absolute necessity to appoint a new Head, and meeting again on 31st December received Mr Inchbald's offer of resignation from the end of July 1904. After discussion with the Board of Education it was agreed he should be paid £50 a year for ten years. The Governors' three point plan was:

1. Appoint a new Head

Advertisements were placed in *The Times*, *Spectator* and *Atheneum* for a man who had to be under 40, and a graduate of a British university. The salary was £100 p.a. with a capitation fee of £3 to be raised to £4 after 7 years' service. There was a house free of rates and taxes, and accommodation for 12 boarders at 50 guineas p.a., exclusive of tuition fees. The number at the School in March 1904 was 60. The intending candidates were also to be told that no claim for compensation would be entertained if the School had to be closed, hardly a show of confidence!

2. Raise extra resources

The Inspectors had said that the tuition fees at a standard rate of £15 a year were as high as *"the school attractions permit"*; the endowment income was going down steadily as capital assets were used e.g. in building a new Tiffin Girls' School at a cost of £15,515 so that the expanding Tiffin Boys' could take over the whole Tiffin site. So, there would have to be a public appeal for fund to improve the buildings with the hope that revenue from a substantial increase in the number of pupils would make it possible to meet running costs.

3. Change the name of the School

"It was resolved that the title "The Kingston Grammar School" be adopted in future instead of the Queen Elizabeth School and that the Board of Education be requested to use such title ... and that it be continued in the future." It proved easier to change the name of the School than to get sufficient funds to improve the premises. Hoping for £4000, the Governors raised £2000 which the *Comet* said was *"the minimum on which the Governors had considered it possible to make do."* This meant the retiring Head would not get, as hoped, a £1000 lump sum as a farewell but only £250; and a new classroom could not be built, though as the *Comet* leader writer pointed out, it would not be needed until there were more pupils anyway (26 March 1904).

Reverend W Elliot Inchbald Departs

Mr Inchbald bade farewell at the Annual Prizegiving on 27th July 1904. He did not mince his words. Apart from external competition,

The whole school outside the new buildings c. 1900

The Chapel was converted into a gymnasium in 1904 and remained as such for over 30 years

"there has been I am sorry to add some hindrance within our own borders, in the shape of indifference and even opposition. This is in my opinion the chief danger with which the School has to contend. I am not the cause of it but I earnestly hope it will cease with my departure. With more local enthusiasm for its reputation and success the School need fear no rivals." (Comet, 30th July 1904)

Is there an echo here of the previous Headmaster's complaint nearly 40 years before, when, writing in the *Comet*, he said that no town councillor had been near the School in 20 years? Certainly the *Comet* had noted on 26th March that the desire to close the School's doors came in the most part *"from the delegates sent to the Governing body by the Corporation of Kingston."*

The School's Missionary Martyr

One other personality associated with the School in Mr Inchbald's time as Headmaster must have a mention. In 1885 the Headmaster appointed a young Cambridge graduate to be senior Maths and Science master. William Humphrey proved to be not just an excellent teacher but an enthusiastic supporter of extra-mural activities, becoming involved in the entertainments and school debates as well as sports. He "lived in" and was responsible for the welfare of the boarders. But after three years he decided to enter the ministry of the Church of England and went off to train at Ridley Hall, Cambridge. After a curacy at Tunbridge Wells he became, in 1890, Principal of Fourah Bay College, Sierra Leone and later Church Missionary Society Secretary for that colony, as well.

He kept in close contact with the School, through letters and photographs. In one of them reproduced in the *Annual Register* for 1891, he commented *"there is one difficulty which I seldom found with the boys at school, and that is how to prevent the students from working too hard. Lights have to be put out at 10.30 and they are always pleading to be allowed to work until midnight. We also have a rule that no-one must get up to work before 4 am."* The College provided Further Education and was linked to Durham University whose exams they took. It therefore came as a tremendous shock when *The Times* of 19th April 1898 reported that Humphrey had been killed in an uprising, decapitated, his head impaled upon a stick, and displayed around the villages.

What had happened was this. The Colonial Governor had imposed a "hut tax" which was extremely unpopular. Some of the local peoples revolted and the lives of CMS missionaries in the Interior seemed at some risk. Humphrey decided to visit three who were at a village called Ro-Gbere. En route his party was ambushed, his servants and carriers fled in fear for their lives, and Humphrey was never seen alive again.

The murder of someone who had been such a popular teacher at the School and who was regarded as "our" missionary sparked off an Appeal in his memory. Sufficient was collected to provide a capital sum to fund an annual prize to be awarded at Speech Day, "The W J Humphrey Memorial Prize for English". It has been presented annually to this day, though it is doubtful if any boy in modern times who has received it has any idea who is being commemorated, or why.

Finding a Successor as Head of KGS

The Governors had no less than 77 applicants for the Headship and selected Reverend Harold Ryley who was Headmaster of Sir Roger Manwood Grammar School, Sandwich. He declined the post. So they turned to their second choice, Mr E N Marshall, BA Cantab who had been six years senior Classics Master at Loretto School, Musselburgh in Scotland. Mr Marshall took up the post for only one year, before moving on *"for personal reasons"*. In fact he had been offered the Headship of Walsall School where he had a very successful time. During his short spell at KGS he did make two important changes, which went some way to meeting the Inspectors' demands. They had said an extra classroom was needed. He turned the boarders' dormitory which was above the main schoolroom into a classroom transferring the boarders to the Headmaster's house. They had said the School needed a gymnasium. He adapted the Lovekyn Chapel to this purpose.

So, in 1904, the School buildings looked like this. Entering by the main door facing London Road just as now, one turned left into the Headmaster's house and right into the School itself. There was also a separate entrance to the house by a side door at the East end of the range. At the back of the house where the Hall now stands there were domestic quarters (single storied) and

The whole school 1904; the Headmaster Edward Marshall insisted on everyone wearing the Scottish uniform of his previous school, Loretto

the Headmaster's garden. Turning right on entry one came to the classrooms. On the ground floor there was the large room which is now the Dining Room and above the room of similar size from which the boarders had been ejected. Later these were both to be divided so as to form four classrooms. In addition there was a small classroom adjoining the main room. The only other buildings were the Chapel Gym and the Chemistry Laboratory, free-standing to the left of the School. To the rear was a gravel playground stretching back to the southern limit of the Quadrangle as it now is. Beyond this and separated from it by a fence was the School Field which ran back to the Fairfield, then as now the limit of the School grounds.

The Governors tried a third time, and selected Reverend Ernest Stowell, BA Queen's College, Oxford who was to remain Headmaster until 1913. Nothing in the records suggests he was a man to set the Thames on fire. Numbers went up to 74 by 1911 and 96 in Mr Stowell's last year 1912-13. The trouble was that boys were still not staying much beyond the age of fifteen. Out of 130 boys who left between 1905 and 1913 whose subsequent career could be traced none went direct from the School to Oxford or Cambridge, only five going to other Universities or University Colleges. On the other hand, some 30 left to enter one of the big London schools such as St Paul's or a boarding school of the public school type. Just after Mr Stowell left a team of four Inspectors concluded in 1914 as follows:

"In the Report of 1903 it was remarked that the School is not inefficient but it is wholly lacking in distinction. Both these statements are still true. The School has no doubt done a useful service as in some sense a Preparatory School and also in providing an education up to matriculation standard for a certain number of boys whose parents have been unable to pay the fees of the more expensive London schools, and at the same time preferred not to send their sons to the Tiffin Boys School because they wished them to learn Latin or for some other reason."

This is not to say that the School stagnated. There were at least four important developments. First, the School finances were put on a much sounder footing. Under a Board of Education Order of 1905 the distribution of the endowment income was changed to give a much larger share to KGS on the grounds that this income was much reduced due to all the buildings financed from the Trust's capital for the two Tiffin Schools. Since 1902 the School had been in receipt of a grant from the Board of Education, but Surrey County Council continued to give only nominal help whereas they paid the full deficit between tuition fees and per capita cost per pupil, in respect of all those who lived in the County, who attended the Tiffin Schools (in 1913 Tiffin Boys' got £1500, Tiffin Girls' £750 and KGS £88). The status of the School also changed under a Board of Education Scheme in 1910 which amended the 1874 settlement. It changed the composition of the Governors to the Mayor, Aldermen and Burgesses of the Borough of Kingston upon Thames. From now on it was to be the Kingston Grammar School Committee of Kingston Council which ran the School right up until 1978, when the School went independent.

Secondly, KGS became increasingly well known as a first-rate Hockey school; in part no doubt this was because no other winter sport was played. Other schools only played hockey in the Spring term as they were wont to point out! It was not just that KGS played much more of the game; the matches in the autumn term were against adult teams. And Old Boys were in evidence at the highest levels of the sport. In the November 1907 edition of the *Kingstonian* founded in June that year to replace the *Register*, defunct since 1902, it is pointed out the School has three current internationals in S H Shoveller, N Nightingale and G Logan, all of whom had been prefects, whilst another four were playing at County level. KGS Old Boys' Hockey Club, later to become the Old Kingstonian HC, was founded at the beginning of the 1908-9 season and was to be one of the leading clubs in the land. (See Chapter 13 for the full story.)

The third event of note was the founding (or refounding) of an Old Boys Association, at a meeting on 16th December 1909. Although the Head, presiding, referred to the Old Kingstonian Society having been in a state of suspended animation for four or five years there seems to be no record of this earlier incarnation. The first of very many annual dinners was held in January 1910 and attended by 26 Old Boys. The Society was to play an important part in the life of the School as the years progressed.

The Great Pageant – July 1909

Whether it was the Headmaster, Chairman of the Governors, Dr Goodman a wealthy local philanthropist, or Dr Finny, Mayor of the Borough and an authority on Kingston's history, who had the idea of a Pageant to celebrate the six-hundredth anniversary of the founding of Lovekyn's Chapel is not clear. But it quickly caught on and became a major event of the town's year. After a commemorative service in Kingston Parish Church at which the Bishop of Kingston gave the sermon, there was a large public luncheon in Nuthall's Restaurant, and the dignitaries then processed on to the site of the Pageant itself. This was held in the grounds of Elmfield, which immediately adjoined the Chapel and originally formed part of the Chapel Warden's garden and orchard. The Pageant consisted of colourful episodes chronicling the history of Chapel and School. And there was an attractive colour brochure. The rain held off and the *Comet* pronounced the Sexcentenary Pageant *"a triumphant success"*, giving it two full pages of broadsheet coverage. Certainly it was a project which brought the Church, the Council and the School into a closer association than they had been before, and raised the School's profile considerably.

So as the Edwardian age drew to a close KGS was, as an academic estab-

W E Finny as Mayor of Kingston 1898; a prominent local historian who researched the origins of the Lovekyn Chapel

lishment, of no distinction but none the less had an assured position within Kingston. There were no more suggestions, from Governors or the Board of Education that its future might be in doubt, and closure a possibility. But if Mr Stowell arrested the downward drift, it was to be his successor who turned things round and set the School on the successful course which it has maintained ever since.

CHAPTER 8

—··◆··—

A School of a Different Kind – C A Howse (1913-1941)

—··◆··—

MR C A HOWSE (CHARLIE HOWSE) came to the School in the autumn term 1913. He had taught as an assistant master at two secondary schools after taking a BA in classics from Clare College, Cambridge, and was only 28 when appointed Head at KGS. Just over a year later in November 1914, when a full Inspection by the Board of Education had, as already mentioned, some pretty negative comments to make about the lack of progress over the previous ten years, there were kindly words for the way the School was being run by the young new Head. *"In matters of order and class discipline the School has markedly improved since he took charge"*; and as for his qualities as a teacher, *"He is a good scholar and a capable teacher, and should do much to raise the standard of work in the School in those subjects for which he is more directly responsible"*. Indeed the Inspectors seem to have taken quite a shine to Mr Howse concluding their comments by saying that *"the School is likely to improve under the present Headmaster."*

They could scarcely have guessed, however just what a transformation was to take place. Returning in 1924 a team of six HMI's gave the School the sort of commendation it had never before received:

"The outstanding fact about the School is that it has trebled its numbers since the last inspection (in 1914) and that this growth which has been rapid during the last few years is still continuing. The growth in numbers has carried with it an improved financial position, better organisation and enhanced possibilities of substantial advanced work at the top. Sufficient time has not elapsed for the full effect of these improved conditions to show themselves, but much ground has been won and the Governors and the Headmaster may be congratulated on the progress which the School has made."

By the time of the next General Inspection, in 1934, the remarks were even more complimentary:

C A Howse, Headmaster
1913–1941

The front of the School in
Headmaster Howse's time

"The development of the School in size, status and efficiency since the appointment of the present Head Master in 1913 is directly due to his unflagging devotion and skilful guidance. He has shown a wise appreciation of its needs and problems and, never sparing himself, sets an inspiring example to boys and Masters .... That service on the staff of this School provides a good professional training is shown by the significant fact that during the Head Master's tenure of office six of his staff have been appointed to Head Masterships. .... During the last 20 years the development of the School in status and efficiency has been continuous."

Presenting this Report to the Governors at a special meeting on 2nd March 1934, the leader of the inspecting team told them that the Head Master was second to none in his devotion to his school which reflected his personality. The Head had won the complete confidence of the Inspectors, the Governors were told. The impression given is of a man whose determination was that nothing would stand in in the way of his almost missionary zeal to make KGS a force to be reckoned with in the world of secondary education. A schoolboy's view from Nick Barnett (1920-1928):

"In my day the Headmaster was Howse, called Charlie behind his back; all the boys and most of the masters were scared stiff of him. But he was a very just man and on one occasion when a master gave me the choice of two hours detention on the actual day of the punishment or to go to the Headmaster, I chose the latter and was allowed to do my two hour stint on the next half-day."

The School in 1914

The new Head took over a school with six full time and four part time staff, and a school roll of 96; five were boarders (this was the last year when there were boarders at the School). Fees were £12 a year for the under 10's, £16-10-0 for 10-12 and £17-5-0 for the over 12s. At the end of his first year, in July 1914 there were 99 pupils but only five were in the sixth form. Six of the boys came from Middlesex, 34 from Kingston, 13 from Surbiton and the others from the rest of Surrey, apart from three Belgian refugees. The Governors awarded a handful of scholarships and Exhibitions; two of each were in payment in the whole School, and in addition ten boys had free places, a condition of the School getting a government grant. The School was organised in seven Forms but as the sixth form was taught with the Remove (what would now be the GCSE year) there were really only six. The subjects taught were:

> English and Literature
> History
> Geography
> French
> German

In class – probably about 1914

Latin – one boy for Greek
Mathematics
Science
Art – in the three lower forms only
Physical Exercises – PE

The School buildings themselves remained far from ideal:

"There are six classrooms providing accommodation for about 110 boys, and a laboratory, whilst the Chapel is utilised as before for the purposes of a gymnasium. This room is too narrow for the purpose and of an old fashioned type. There is no washing accommodation available for the assistant staff, and the staffroom is also utilised both for singing and as a place in which boys can take their midday meal. There is no proper cloakroom; coats and caps are hung in the corridor, or in a shed in the playground provided with a stove which stands in need of repair."

(Inspection Report 1914)

There are no details of examination results in the Report and the issues of the *Kingstonian* for 1912-1917 are missing from the Library. The Inspectors' comment is brief. *"So far as the actual standard of attainment is concerned it may be said that while recent results in the Cambridge Senior Local Examination were poor those in the Junior Local were quite creditable."* In the sixth form four boys had passed the Senior Local of whom three were studying for entrance to the Civil Service.

KGS and the First World War

Mr Howse had barely been at the School for a year when, on 4th August 1914 war was declared against Germany. Without the School magazine there are only glimpses of School life from other sources. Masters went off to the War and four of them were killed on active service. Three lady teachers were employed, though they seem to have been treated on sufferance. Recording their departure in 1919 the *Kingstonian* did not even give their names, but just said: *"At the end of the term we said goodbye to the three ladies who have been helping us during the war."* A Cadet Corps was formed in 1915 at a cost of £155 for equipment, and parents were expected to contribute five shillings a term to the Corps funds. The Corps was part of the 1st Cadet Battalion of the East Surreys which also had Tiffin's and three other schools in it, with the whole Battalion under the command of the Head, Major Howse. There was the usual round of Field Days with compass exercises, and mock battles. The highlight was the Annual Camp from 1916 onwards, on Marlborough Common. There were drills, cross-country races, sports, night operations, lectures and in the evenings concerts, including one given each year for the inhabitants of Marlborough in their Town Hall, a thoroughly enjoyable fortnight, apparently.

Then of course there was the drive for National Savings to support the war effort, reported periodically to the Governors. In March 1917, for instance, the Headmaster told them that over £100 had already been raised that year from pupils. The following year saw nearly £1000 raised on Tank Day and in the Feed the Guns Campaign. A collection of a rather more mysterious nature was reported that year to the Governors, when the Head told them that, as desired by the Board of Education in the circular recently issued by them, the boys had collected a number of horse chestnuts for the Ministry of Munitions.

A feature that was perhaps less expected of the war years was the rapid increase in the number of pupils. By June 1915 the total was 100, in January 1916 the number on the roll was 122 and in October 1916 it had risen to 137 and Mr Howse informed the Governors that the School was now full. None the less more boys were admitted over the next four years, the roll reaching 165 in 1919. In part this meteoric rise may have been due to the new Headmaster's burgeoning reputation, but it may also have owed a lot to parents preferring to have their boys at a local school during such uncertain times rather than going into London to schools like St Paul's, or away to boarding schools.

If the war did not greatly affect life at the School its impact on generations of Old Boys was enormous. The details of those who served in the Forces are set out in the December 1919 issue of the *Kingstonian*. No less than 237 Old Boys had seen military service. In relation to the size of the School this was remarkable, for during the late Victorian and early Edwardian years, which provided the young men of the Great War period, the annual intake of pupils

The officers of the Cadet Corps, 1917 Major Howse, C.O. seated at centre

CHRISTMAS GREETINGS
FROM THE 19ᵗʰ DIVISION ∴ ∴

The back of the card was inscribed:
"To Pips from Bundy. To commemorate the first Christmas to be spent in peace for four years"
St Leger, France 17 December 1918

was only 15 or so each year. Of the 237, a total of 33 were killed by the enemy, or died of wounds. And the roll of gallantry awards was one in which any school could take pride.

Two Old Kingstonians received the DSO. No less than 14 were awarded the Military Cross and another three the Military Medal which was the equivalent award for "other ranks". Six were "Mentioned in Despatches", and there were foreign awards as well, a Russian Military Cross, a Serbian Gold Medal and a French Croix de Guerre. So all told there were 28 awards for valour. Two of those who fought in the War were to have distinguished careers which stemmed from their experiences in this conflict, Gerald Gibbs and R C (Bob) Sherriff.

2nd Lieutenant Gerald Gibbs, RAF

By the time he reached the age of 22 Gerald Gibbs had shot down ten enemy aircraft, won the Military Cross with two bars as well as the Croix de Guerre and been appointed to the Légion d'honneur. His exploits were of *Boy's Own Paper* proportions as one of the RFC's early flying aces. He had left KGS in 1912 when he was sixteen, joined the Wiltshire Regiment as a private in 1914, was commissioned whilst serving in France and then head hunted by the Royal Flying Corps. In his autobiography he claimed it was the eight shillings a day extra pay that proved irresistible. But he was a born airman. He flew solo after just one hour and after ten hours in the air was an instructor. He stayed on in the RAF after the war ended and rose to the top echelons. In the Battle of Britain he was No 2 at Fighter Command's embattled No 11 Group defending south east England, and ended the war as Mountbatten's chief staff officer at Supreme Allied Headquarters, South East Asia. His last two appointments were as chief military advisor to the UK delegation to the United Nations (1948-51) and as the last RAF officer to be Commander in Chief of the Indian Air Force (1951-54). Air Marshall Sir Gerald Gibbs, KBE, CIE, MC died in 1992.

Captain R C Sherriff, East Surreys

Having left school in 1913, where he had been Captain of Rowing and of Cricket, R C (Bob) Sherriff became a clerk with the Sun Assurance Company. At the outbreak of war he enlisted in the 9th East Surrey Regiment. He was commissioned, served at Vimy and Loos and was severely wounded at Ypres. He was discharged, and returned to insurance work. One of his hobbies was play-writing and in 1928 he wrote *Journey's End*, a play with an all male cast set in a dug-out on the Western Front. Nothing like it had been seen before. It ran for 594 performances in the West End with Laurence Olivier in the lead, and by the time it came off had been produced in 20 other countries. As *The Times* put it *"a great play, no; a great war play, yes; a play fulfilling what is surely a great purpose in bringing home to audiences*

everywhere what modern warfare is really like". Bob Sherriff had a string of later successes including *Badgers Green, Home at Seven,* and *The White Carnation,* wrote for radio and television and was the scriptwriter for many films, amongst them, *The Invisible Man, St Helena, Lady Hamilton,* and most famously, *The Dambusters.* But it is for *Journey's End,* still regularly revived, that he will be best remembered.

Bob Sherriff never married and lived, in his later years, alone in his large house, Rosebriars, at Esher. He was a benefactor over very many years to KGS and particularly to the Rowing Club, most of whose boats were purchased through his generosity, and whose social club still bears his name. In his will, he provided that the royalties on all his works should be shared between the Scouts' Association and the School. Even now this brings in two or three thousand pounds every year to the School.

R C Sherriff, FSA, FRSL, died in November 1975.

By way of a footnote, *Journey's End* was in the late 20's regarded as something of a national symbol, not just a good war play. The *Kingstonian* for December 1929 states *"Recently the MSS of the play was sold, after presentation to the League of Nations Union, for £1500. The purchaser brought the MSS for the Nation and Sir Edward Lutyens is to design a special casket for it."*

Memorial Service

Bene agere ac lætari.

In Memory of

Old Boys and Masters of Kingston Grammar School

who fell in the Great War,

held at the

Parish Church of All Saints,

Kingston-upon-Thames.

✠

Followed by the

Unveiling of the Mural Tablet

at the School.

✠

Sunday, 19th September, 1920, at 3 p.m.

IN MEMORIAM – 1920 Memorial Service and unveiling of Mural Tablet at the school.

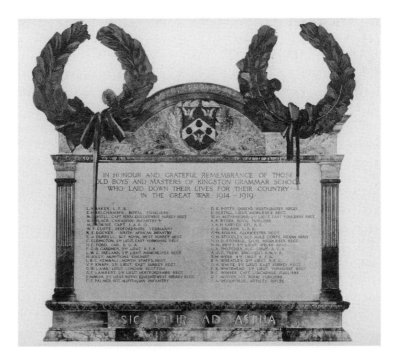

The number of boys in the School continued to increase rapidly after the end of the War. From 162 in October 1918 the number rose to 280 in 1923, by which time 18 were 16 and over, the basis for a respectable sixth form. The average age of leaving had risen to 15 years and 9 months. And there was now a serious attempt to bring into the School able boys from the elementary schools. In 1918 there were 3 half fee scholarships and 6 free place scholarships. Four of these came from Merton C of E Junior School, but the Board of Education concurred in the restriction for the future of free places to the area served by the School. In 1920 boys from Elm Road, St Paul's Kingston and Tolworth Council School are listed in the minutes of the Council's Secondary Education Committee as getting free places. Acceptance of a free place, at the Tiffin Schools as well as at KGS, involved an undertaking not to leave before the end of the school year in which the pupil reached the age of 16. The penalty was paying to the Governors *"the equivalent of one year's tuition fees at the rate payable by ordinary pupils at the School at the time of such withdrawal."* Tuition fees were then running at £25 a year.

This explosion in numbers put a severe strain on the accommodation for teaching purposes which was resolved in an unusual way. The Headmaster would give up his house, move out and find his own accommodation in return for a living out allowance of £120 a year. This would be added to his salary of £150 a year, and to a capitation fee of £2-10-0 per pupil per term provided that the total did not exceed £900 a year. If he wished he could at any time apply to receive instead the appropriate salary for the Headmaster of a Surrey Secondary School. Thus at a stroke the size of the School buildings was increased by about a third (minutes of Secondary Education Committee 28 July 1921). Already in 1920 an ex-army hut had been erected and in 1922, a further Repair Fund was launched for the Lovekyn Chapel raising £750, a notable contributor being Leonard Bentall whose store on Clarence Street was expanding rapidly.

Numbers continued to rise and peaked at 362 in 1926, slipping back to 318 in 1930, due the HMI report said to the lower birth rates of the war period. By 1934 though they had recovered to 344. Numbers were scarcely to change after this until the expansion after the Second World War. New buildings more than kept pace with the increase in the numbers of boys. In 1924 a new block was built comprising a physics laboratory and two classrooms, whilst in 1927 the Great Hall was formally opened on 7th May (Speech Day) by the Bishop of Kingston. Extra classrooms above the 1924 block were added, so that the Quad then appeared much as it does today. Of the new Hall, certainly the most distinguished school building pre-war, the Editor of the *Kingstonian* wrote, in December 1929 *"Gone are the days when we all crammed ourselves into the partitioned rooms on the west side of the old building, when latecomers found there was little or no room in which to squeeze themselves before the bell stopped."*

The Great Hall, opened in 1927

The Chemistry Laboratory

The rooms referred to are those which are now the school dining room. There was more to come. Major Percy, Chairman of the Governors, obtained funds to improve the Chemistry Laboratory and add another classroom. Then in 1937 the Chapel finally ceased to be what the Inspectors had always regarded as a travesty of a gymnasium when the present gym at the Fairfield end of the site, beyond the Cage was built, the first of many additional buildings at that end.

Even the Chapel at last received the national recognition it deserved when in 1927 the Council received a letter from HM Office of Works:

"I am directed by the First Commissioner of His Majesty's Works etc to inform you that the Ancient Monuments Board of England have reported to the Commissioners that Lovekyn's Chantry Chapel (or St Mary Magdelen's Chapel, Kingston upon Thames, in the County of Surrey), of which the Corporation of Kingston upon Thames is understood to be the owner, is a monument the preservation of which is of national importance.

The Commissioners will accordingly include this monument in the lists which they are required to prepare and publish by section 12 of the Ancient Monuments Consolidation and Amendment Act 1913 ...."

That this letter was addressed to the Corporation, not to the School, reflects the fact that right up to 1977 KGS was governed by a Council Committee, the Kingston Grammar School Sub-Committee of the Secondary Education Committee of the Council.

Academic Excellence

This had never been a problem for KGS since, apart from the glory days of Wooddeson in the 18th Century, the School had never aspired to such excellence. Great at hockey, but not much else, would have been a fair comment when Howse took over in 1913. Academically it was *"not inefficient but wholly lacking in distinction"* as the HMI report of November 1914 put it. Interestingly it was just 7 years after Charlie Howse took over that the first significant academic success was obtained, i.e. by someone who was eleven when the new Head came to the School. In 1920 Ubee became the first boy to gain a Surrey County Major scholarship, and in celebration the School was given a half day holiday. That same year three boys gained Higher School Certificates. On the strength of this new found success the Chairman of Governors said the fees could go up from £17-50 to £20 a year. Ubee's was the first of 22 County Major scholarships to be won over the next 20 years. In 1927 came the first Open university scholarship, to Imperial College, London to be followed by another six during the 1930s. But it was of course not just such achievements that mattered. At the 1938 Speech Day, the Headmaster in his Report on the year commented that there were now 22 Old Boys at the Universities and no fewer than 20 boys had gained school certificates with 100 of their papers reaching Credit standard.

Speech Day in the Great Hall, opened 1927

The Chapel officially recognised as a national monument in 1927

To what should this success story be attributed? Above all it was because of the drive (some would say drivenness) of an outstanding Head who took every opportunity to advance the interests of the School. He had a knack for picking good staff. As the 1934 HMI Report puts it *"though the staff includes no individuals of particular distinction it is as a body well qualified, both academically and in teaching power. Of the 16 masters, 10 are Honours men and eleven are graduates of Oxford or Cambridge."* With more teachers and more boys, not to mention vastly improved accommodation, came the opportunity for a wider and more stimulating curriculum all of which made the School more attractive to parents. Greater demand meant that it was possible to put up fees (at a time of little inflationary pressure). The annual fee which was £17-5s in 1914 had risen to £28 in 1927. Equally important, Middlesex and Surrey County Councils finally agreed in 1934 to pay a proper capitation fee of three pounds a year in respect of each of their boys at the School. The HMI's reckoned this would amount to £200 from Middlesex and £300 from Surrey each year, as much as the whole of the School's endowment income, £497 in the year 1932-33. It meant that the School which was £1020 in debt over the three years to March 1932 could look to a credit balance in future years. Above all, success bred success. KGS was no longer regarded as a "posher" but more expensive yet less effective school than Tiffin Boys'. And the Head lost no opportunity of emphasising that his school was now in a Senior league. The School rowed in the Public School IV's at Reading and Marlow regattas; the prestigious annual cricket fixture with the MCC was gained in 1931. Continental Hockey tours started in 1926 and in the 1927 Public Schools' Hockey International the School had two caps. From being a very indifferent local grammar school KGS was gaining a significant position among its peers. The full story of sporting achievements between the wars is told in Chapter 14.

In small matters too the picture is of a school on the move. In 1922 it was decided there should be an Honours Board. And the prizes at Speech Day were, now that there some worthwhile academic results, being presented by people of distinction. In the five years up to 1938 these were the Lord Mayor of London, the High Sheriff of Surrey, Sir George Perry, Kingston's MP, the Bishop of Southwark, and Sir Thomas Inskip, Minister for Defence Co-ordination. No one could say Charlie Howse failed to give KGS a high profile.

In fact there seems to have been only one major criticism of the School's facilities, and that was of the Library which as late as 1934 was still getting a books grant of only £5 a year. The visiting HMIs' comment was that *"the selection of books has been sensibly made but no subject is generously represented and in view of the amount of advanced work in the School the apparatus of scholarship is poorer than might reasonably be expected"*. The annual grant immediately went up from £5 to £50 according to the Head's annotated copy of the Report. What's more, the Head was authorised to purchase a set of the *Encyclopaedia Britannica* for £18-12-6d and this was swiftly followed by a KGS Council Committee resolution to add a set of the *Children's Encyclopaedia* to the Library at a cost of a further £7-7-0. An improved Library service was well under way.

The School Community

Even in its darkest days the School had a reputation for having a real concern for the well-being of its scholars. It may well be this factor that enabled it to continue to attract pupils even when the academic results were far from excellent. For some parents a friendly, caring community was no doubt of importance.

In 1903 Inspectors commented that *"the boys seem to be well cared for. The Headmaster takes much interest in their games and other pursuits and, so far as discipline, order and physical well-being go, no criticism or unfavourable comment is made."* Subsequent Reports were also affirmative, with the one for 1934 saying that *"the general behaviour and bearing of the boys at lessons and outside the classroom made an excellent impression .... Records of all the school activities which are unusually comprehensive and varied are found in the School magazine".*

By the mid 1930s there certainly was a wide range of extra-mural activities in addition to a burgeoning sports programme (see Chapter 14). Long established school clubs like the Gibbon Society flourished. The *Kingstonian* reported that in the Spring Term 1923, the Society was debating the influence of the cinema and had concluded that *"it tended to foster a growing craving for pleasure and a shallow sentimentality, especially among the lower orders".* That same term saw a lantern lecture on the delights of Oxford and in the summer a *"breaking up sing-song".* The members took a more reasoned view a year later when they emphatically rejected a resolution that *"The principles of fascism are beneficial to Europe."* But the Society found itself increasingly in competition with the Archaeological Society founded in 1927 which was involved in a wide range of cultural and historical activities. In 1937 the issue came to a head when it was reported in the Magazine that it *"has been decided that henceforth the Archaeological Society shall be known as the Gibbon Society.... The name is thus transferred from the Debating Society, which will adopt another title."* In fact the former Gibbon Society continued as the Debating Society, to debate such subjects as, in 1939, *"That the modern age is degenerate"* and *"That the present inequality of riches is justified".* In the same year they visited the Houses of Parliament, and the Jubilee Exhibition at the LCC; and had lectures on Medieval Church Architecture and History through Postage Stamps.

Music and drama began to have a more prominent place in the School, encouraged perhaps by the purchase, in 1924 of *"a Gramophone of excellent tone and construction. It is hoped a weekly concert lasting 35 minutes after school will be attractive."* (The *Kingstonian*.) 1927 saw the nucleus of a School orchestra being formed but it seemed to have a somewhat intermittent life; the comment on the Christmas entertainment at the Assembly Rooms was *"In the Intervals Mr R E Nicholls conducted the orchestra which he so kindly assembles for these occasions."* (The *Kingstonian*.) Also in 1927 a Dramatic Club was formed. This too seems to have taken a while to become established, but in 1935 the School for the first time attempted the performance of a three act play, a light comedy of *"youthful High spirits and anti-parental activities called the Rising Generation".*

Some School Societies are ephemeral, depending on the enthusiasm and knowledge of one or two people and others, like the Wireless Society busy in 1923 building a set which would they said consist of a loosely coupled tuner employing crystal verification, simply got overtaken by events. The Meteorological Society's weather station seems to have ceased in the mid-40s having been established in 1920. Its work very much impressed the Inspectors in 1934. *"Some 20 boys act as observers and maintain continuity of readings throughout the holidays. Rainfall records are sent annually to the British Rainfall Association and forecasts are supplied weekly to the local paper, The Surrey Comet, a creditable enterprise."*

But two of the new societies were to have a long life, the Cercle Français and the Christian Union. The former which started life in 1924 was concerned to encourage all things French with play-reading, concerts and theatre visits. Debates were in French of course and members were told that it would help them conquer their bashful feeling of speaking in public in a foreign language if they came to meetings with a speech prepared beforehand. Like all societies the French Circle had to compete with the demands of school discipline. Two meetings in the Spring Term 1927 had to be put off *"owing to the greater attraction of Late Detention."*

KGS Christian Union made a very modest start in July 1933 with meetings that lasted about half an hour every Monday evening and a pre-school Prayer Meeting every Thursday. Whilst fading away during the war, it was revived in 1948, though it was not until the 1950s that the Christian Union became a powerful influence through its Houseparties and summer camps. These have continued every year to attract pupils in large numbers to this day.

This period also saw the introduction of overseas school visits. The *Kingstonian* records that at Easter 1928, for the third year in succession a party from the School led by Mr Lodge set off for a holiday on the Continent, at Bruges. There are records of subsequent trips to Switzerland and Paris. In fact from 1926 onwards, right up to the War, Easter trips to the Continent were a regular feature of school life.

No account of KGS at this time could omit reference to the Cadet Corps, which was a major influence on so many boys. It is difficult to do that role justice because by its very nature it was largely repetitive year on year. Taking a year more less at random, in 1924, 17 boys went to the Summer Camp at Winchester (the Public Schools' Cadet Camp), which attracted over a thousand boys. The School sent a bigger contingent to the 1925 Camp; 32 boys attended a camp of over 1300 at Cheltenham. If Camp was the highlight of the year, during term time there were field days, night operations, shooting and House drill competitions, the smartest Cadet competition and of course the Annual Inspection which took place on the Fairfield. Inter-school operations took place in Richmond Park with the School Corps engaged alongside Richmond Hill School, Tiffin School and Rutlish School. Perhaps the account of Field Day on 20th March 1925 will bring back memories of such events in the life of Cadet Corps members over the years.

"A halt was called for lunch, but among the junior cadets there arose a difference of opinion concerning neutral zones and it took all the fatherly admonitions of the platoon Sergeants and the fists of the section commanders to prevent them fighting an action there and then. After lunch the enemy slipped away and took up a final position amongst trees, sandhills and ditches. .... The attack then lined the bank of a sunken road and the signal was given to go over the top. However a long time was spent scrambling up the steep bank and reorganising the section on the top to the accompaniment of a pitiful display of covering fire. At last the attacking force was artistically displayed along a forward slope being raked by machine gun and rifle fire. When the charge was sounded forty tired and heated cadets and their NCOs went forward in the approved "up guard and at em" style. About ten succeeded in reaching the enemy's main line whilst the remainder were busy extricating themselves from ditches and thorn bushes. Such of the defence as were not enfilading the remainder of the attack, counter-attacked these ten "heroes". The cease fire however cut short their amicable intentions; and the field day was brought to a close, everybody, except, of course, the attackers, agreeing that victory lay in the hands of the defence." (Kingstonian, July 1925)

But perhaps the most important feature introduced into school life was the House system which the Headmaster put into effect just a year after his arrival, in 1914. Every boy was allocated to a House, one of three in the first instance, Lovekyn, Walworth, or Queen Elizabeth, with a fourth House, Taverner added in 1921 as the School numbers increased. Inter-House competitions at Junior and Senior levels all contributing points towards the annual House Championship gave many boys who might never represent the School the chance to do their bit, and feel valued. Similarly the introduction of House Colours for those who represented their House with credit provided an accessible goal for the less gifted in sports. And there was always the possibility of being mentioned in despatches, the termly House Notes which appeared in the *Kingstonian*. As well as accolades, House Notes, usually compiled by the House Captain and House Secretary often contained admonition directed toward the laggards:

"Those members of the House who feel they are not doing as much as they could are urged to give the Cadet Corps a trial. Many would do so if they had energy enough to make the initial effort of enlisting."

"Reviewing our position we can say that too much reliance is on a few boys. Greater enthusiasm for all House activities must be shown by a larger number of boys."

"We have had more than our fair share of being in the bottom position in the House Championship. Nearly every boy will find that he can take part in at least one of the House activities; we urge every member to pull his weight."

Old Kingstonians

The Old Kingstonian Hockey Club, dormant in the war years, was revived in 1919 as was the Old Boys' Association itself. The Hockey Club, soon to become the Old Kingstonians (the OKs), was to be a dominant force in English senior hockey for half a century. By the 1926-27 season they were running no less than five Eleven's. Although this put the activities of the Old Boys' Association (the OKA) somewhat in the shade, the Association was very active in the period up to the Second World War. There was an OK Lawn Tennis Club, and in 1933 an OK, HGN Lee, played in the Davis Cup team. The OK Tennis Club expired in 1936. An OK Rugby Football Club, started in 1935 also had a short life as the School only took the game up for a few years before reverting to hockey for both winter terms.

Away from the sports scene altogether there were interesting developments. The *Old Kingstonian Magazine* was founded in 1933 and carried on till outbreak of war. There was even an OK clubhouse at the Poplars in Fassett Road, Kingston. *"The Club provides the usual attractions, except billiards"* (a table was later added). *"It is open to members of the Association on weekdays from 4pm onwards and on Sundays from 12-2 and again in the evening."* Unfortunately members failed to give the venture their support, attendance was poor and the Club closed its doors in March 1936.

Like most alumni associations the OKs had a distinctive tie and indeed a blazer, with badge. There was an Annual General Meeting, an Annual Dinner and the Association began, in 1922, a pattern of donations to the School which continues to this day. Their first gift was £5 towards the cost of a House Challenge Cup; in 1998 the latest donation, towards the 1998 School Appeal, was a magnificent £10,000. Help of a different sort came in 1935 when the Association set up a Careers Bureau: *"A number of Old Boys representing a variety of professions, trades and businesses have consented to interview or communicate with any boy from the School who may be interested."* It was also agreed books dealing with Careers should be presented to the School.

A Change of Headmaster

At the end of the autumn half term break in 1940 the School's Headmaster since 1913, Charlie Howse, simply did not return to School. He had it seems suffered a nervous breakdown. He never did come back, and the minutes of the Kingston Grammar School Sub-Committee meeting on 11th March 1941 make sad reading:

"HEADMASTERS RETIREMENT. A letter was submitted from the Board of

Education notifying the award of disablement allowances to Mr C A Howse and a letter was submitted from Mr Howse with regard to his retirement through ill health.

The Education Secretary reported that he had informed the Board of Education that full salary had been paid up to 31st January 1941. The Chairman referred to the past services of the Headmaster and it was resolved that a letter be sent to Mr Howse regretting this retirement had been enforced through ill health, expressing the Governors appreciation of his long and devoted service, for the success of the school and extending him best wishes for a long and happy period of retirement."

So, at the age of 58, this distinguished Headmaster who had, in his 28 years at the helm, transformed KGS from a school which seemed to have no worthwhile future into a very good day grammar school that could hold its own with its neighbours, simply slipped away from the scene. Had he been able to see his time out, retiring after the war, what accolades he might have received.

But the Grammar School Committee had to decide what should be done about appointing a successor. Their conclusion was that Mr E W James, Senior Assistant Master, be offered the post of Acting Headmaster till 31st March 1942 continuing thereafter if circumstances as determined by the Governors called for that step. (In fact he was confirmed as the permanent Head in 1942.)

CHAPTER 9

——··◆··——

The School in the 1940s

——··◆··——

The Second World War

THE OUTBREAK OF WAR in September 1939 certainly affected life at the School, but from the pupils' point of view, rather less than might be expected. Younger masters, 9 in all went off to join the Forces and of course hundreds of Old Boys joined up over the next five years. But the School was never evacuated and though numbers dropped to a little over 200 in 1940, they were back to 430 by September 1944. That summer did see one school evacuation when 30 boys from the first year forms went off to Fenton, in the Potteries to avoid the V1 and V2 rocket attacks. The 30 left Kingston in mid June, and 28 were back for the start of the autumn term, the culture shock proving just too much.

Lessons were, of course, often interrupted by air raid warnings when the School migrated to the newly built shelters at the Fairfield Road end of the site but otherwise continued as usual and the full curriculum was taught. The Higher School Certificate exams (A levels) were held in the boiler room under the Head's study! By great good fortune none of the buildings was hit by a bomb, though blast took out plenty of windows. The Chapel was unscathed and there was no major damage at the Dinton Road Sports Field. There the full range of House matches – hockey and cricket – continued, and the 1st Elevens continued with a strong array of fixtures, the School sporting year as always culminating in the full day match against the MCC.

Whilst Speech Day had to be abandoned (as was the award of school prizes), and the *Kingstonian* became an annual instead of termly publication, school activities continued, though in a slightly lower key. The French Circle never closed down and by February 1944 drama was back with a performance of Bernard Shaw's *Androcles and the Lion*. Not surprisingly the Cadet Corps went from strength to strength; and there was one entirely new activity, the Harvest Camp. An extract from the report of the 1943 Camp which appeared in the November issue of the *Kingstonian* gives the feel of it.

KINGSTON GRAMMAR SCHOOL.

Governors:

The Education Committee of the Borough of Kingston-upon-Thames.

Education Office:

Guildhall, Kingston-upon-Thames.

Staff:

E. W. H. JAMES, M.Sc. (*Headmaster*), Manchester.

H. W. A. WADLEY, M.A. (*Second Master*), Selwyn College, Cambridge (Mathematics).

M. E. BROWN, M.A., Queen's College, Oxford (Classics).

H. J. ELLIS, M.A., Emmanuel College, Cambridge (Mathematics).

F. J. FIELD, B.A., St. Edmund Hall, Oxford (English).

G. B. FORGE, B.A., London.

A. B. GRIFFITHS, B.A., King's College, London (French).

G. E. HARTLEY, B.A., St. Catherine's College, Cambridge.

E. G. LOCK, M.A., Pembroke College, Oxford (History).

F. MARTIN, M.A., Fitzwilliam House, Cambridge (Form II.).

R. E. NICHOLLS, M.A., Ph.D., Queens' College, Cambridge (French).

V. PACKER, M.A., Queens' College, Cambridge (Science).

A. D. ROBINSON, B.A., Clare College, Cambridge (Chemistry).

R. ROEBUCK, B.A., Queen's College, Oxford (Classics).

J. W. SANDERS, B.A., University College, London (English).

P. R. THOMAS, B.A., Selwyn College, Cambridge.

C. S. TAYLOR, B.A., St. John's College, Oxford (Form I.).

C. MARTIN, Mus. Bac., Oxford (Music).

A. F. PERRY, A.R.C.A., South Kensington (Art).

KINGSTON GRAMMAR SCHOOL.

KINGSTON GRAMMAR SCHOOL has its origin in the remote past; documents have been found which prove that it was in existence in 1264. Queen Elizabeth refounded it in 1561, giving it the buildings and endowment of the Lovekyn Chantry Chapel suppressed by Henry VIII. Hence it was known at one period of its existence as Queen Elizabeth's School.

The School is a Public School, preparing for Business Life, the Professions, the Army, the Civil Service, and the Universities and is provided with a first-rate equipment and staff. The School offers a sound education for the average boy, as well as excellent facilities for advanced work.

Boys are admitted at the age of 9 and may stay until they are 19. Boys of 8 may be accepted if found to be sufficiently advanced.

FEES.

Tuition (per Term) - - -	£9	6	8
Entrance - - - -	£1	1	0
Extra—Instrumental Music -	£2	2	0

During such periods as two or more brothers are in attendance at the School together, there will be a reduction in the fees of the second brother of £1 a term and of the third of £2 a term.

The above fees are payable in advance to the Borough Treasurer, Guildhall, Kingston-upon-Thames. Tuition fees include all subjects of instruction, together with stationery and games. Parents are asked to pay a voluntary 5/- a term towards games expenses.

Class Text Books (costing between 30/- and £3 per annum) are supplied at the School, and the account is forwarded at the end of term.

The work of the Preparatory Department is based on a thorough knowledge of English and Arithmetic, and other subjects are added at various stages.

The School Prospectus, 1941

E W H James, Headmaster
1941–49, and previously Second
Master 1926–1941

"The camp which lasted for six weeks was situated on the South Downs near Slindon in Sussex. Forty-four boys attended the camp and they all enjoyed the work, which varied from tractor driving to tree felling.

Much of the success of the camp was due to the generous help given by Mrs Robinson and Mrs Hyde who worked wonders in the camp kitchen and turned out first-class meals. The fact that most of the boys gained weight while in camp is excellent testimony to their efforts.

The work done by the boys on the farms was greatly appreciated by the farmers who all expressed the wish that the School should hold its 1944 harvest camp at Slindon."

At the first Speech Day after the war, on 21st November 1945, the Headmaster, by then Mr 'Jimmie' James, commented on the School's academic achievements during the period from 1940 to 1945. In spite of all the difficulties, the School stood on what he called good and improving ground. In the five years 47 boys had sat for the Higher School Certificate (predecessor to A Level) and 40 passed. On these results 12 County Major Scholarships were awarded and the four gained in 1944 were the School's best ever results. At School Certificate level (the equivalent of the GCSE exams) 110 out of 125 candidates had been successful. In short the School's pre-war standards had been maintained, despite the turnover in staff and the absence of some of the best teachers. Nine of the staff and over 500 Old Boys served with the forces, at least 14 gallantry awards had been gained, and one master and 57 old boys had made the supreme sacrifice.

As for the Old Boys, both the Hockey Club and the Old Kingstonian Association suspended activities for the duration of hostilities.

'Jimmie' James had come to KGS in 1921 as Senior Science master with an MSc from Victoria University, Manchester having qualified as a teacher in 1911. He served in the Army from 1915 to 1919. From 1926 he was Second Master, and with a solid down to earth no-nonsense approach to schoolmastering he provided an excellent foil to the brilliant if slightly brittle style of the Head. Never without his pipe, stolid and not, he would himself admit, very imaginative, the qualities he said he valued most were a sense of tradition, loyalty and service. He was well suited to see the School through the stormy years of the war, though at any other time his appointment might have raised eyebrows. His laid back style as Head was exemplified by the fact that his first task each day after taking Assembly was to complete *The Times* crossword! And he told his successor that an hour's nap after lunch was an important part of his routine, pointing to the large basket chair in his Study. He had never expected to become Head, being only two years younger than Charlie Howse; but called on in an emergency when steadiness rather than more exciting qualities was what was called for, he did a good job. He was to retire in 1949.

Flight Lieutenant Denis Spotswood

Amongst the many Old Boys who gave their country distinguished service in the Wars was Denis Spotswood. At KGS from 1926 to 1932 he left school after getting his School Certificate, having rowed in the First IV that won the Public Schools Fours at the Reading Regatta in 1932. He does not seem to have belonged to the Cadet Corps, but he enlisted in the RAF, being commissioned as a Pilot Officer in 1936. Serving as a pilot he gained the DFC in 1942 and the DSO in 1943, when he was Officer Commanding No. 500 County of Kent Squadron. By the end of the War he was on Lord Mountbatten's staff at the Supreme Allied Command HQ, South-East Asia. The next 28 years saw him rise to the very top post in the RAF. Spells commanding RAF Fighter Stations, amongst other postings, were followed by him becoming Commandant of the RAF College Cranwell, 1958 to 1961; By then he was an Air Commodore and his subsequent career culminated in the role of Chief of the Air Staff from 1971 to 1974, with the rank of Air Chief Marshal. Sir Denis Spotswood, GCB, CBE, DSO, DFC retired in 1974, a Marshal of the Royal Air Force.

A School Kitchen and School Dinners

In a Memorandum submitted to the Governors, the Kingston Grammar School Committee, on 21st June 1941 the Headmaster stated:

"having been approached by several parents on this question largely owing to the high price of restaurant meals and the present difficulty of a satisfactory sandwich meal at mid-day, parents as a body were circularised to obtain their views. Of 240 enquiries, 180 desired some canteen system to be introduced, 33 (mostly parents whose boys are able to get home at mid-day) did not and some 35 did not reply. It was made clear that this would cost money, 10d or 1/- per meal being mentioned as a likely figure and that such meal would be of the usual British Restaurant type, i.e. nutritious but with little or no choice of dishes."

The decision was to go ahead adapting *"the cloakroom on the right of the main entrance to the building ... The two classrooms adjacent to the proposed kitchen could be utilised for dining purposes."* This is the current dining area, though in fact because school numbers rose rapidly again from 1942 onwards the school hall was utilised for many years leaving the classrooms referred to for teaching purposes. The reference to British Restaurants is to the nation-wide network of Government sponsored restaurants where for a shilling anyone could get a two course meal, without sacrificing any ration coupons. They were very popular and continued for several years after the war. (Rationing be it remembered only ended in 1952.)

The autumn term saw the beginning of the KGS luncheon service. A cook, paid 37/6d a week and three assistants at 30/6d a week did the cooking and serving of the meals. From then on School Meals have been a permanent feature of school life, though they are now provided by a catering firm, under contract and from a larger and completely re-equipped kitchen which was designed in 1995. The initial charge was 10d (roughly 4p) but it was later reduced to 7d (3p)!

During the 1930s the School caretaker used to sell, at break time, doughnuts and Milky Ways from a window looking into the Quad, but a more sophisticated schoolboy source of refreshment was to hand right through the war and indeed until 1949. This was "The Cabin", a tiny cafe or perhaps den might be a better description. This small shop was the unofficial Tuck Shop for KGS boys. It was just down the road towards the town, the other side of the Almshouses. The Cabin's proprietor, Mrs Heath, dispensed her own brew of fizzy drink, variously coloured syrups being mixed on the spot with carbonated water at a penny or tuppence a glass. Mrs Heath had succeeded a lady who had a shop on Hawks Passage which according to Cowan (op.cit.) was at the turn of the century known as Betty Pies Alley, to the boys at least, because she was famed for her gingerbread, nuts, mulberry pies and custards. Since the days of The Cabin the School has for many years run its own highly successful tuck shop on site.

Post War Recovery

The immediate post war years saw little change in the School. As Mr James regularly complained, no permissions were forthcoming to erect new buildings. Without more teaching space the School could expand neither in numbers nor in the curriculum. Exam results, which had never worsened, stayed good. In 1949, the Head's last year, there was one State Scholarship and three Surrey County Major scholarships; ten boys got the Higher School Certificate, and 35 their Oxford and Cambridge School Certificate. In these immediate post war years it was the community life of the School that began to be renewed. The *Kingstonian* records the progress. The Debating Society held four debates in the school year 1945-46, and contentious ones too. *"That the entire Jewish population should be confined to Palestine or another suitable area"* was one and *"That independence should be granted to India immediately"* was another. The Gibbon Society was refounded on a pre-war basis at a meeting held on 25th November 1946. The first visit, to the Exhibition of the King's Pictures, was held the next month. A Chess Society was formed and played friendly matches against neighbouring schools. The *Kingstonian* reverted to its pre-war pattern, appearing every term from November 1947 onwards instead of once a year. The same year also saw the founding of the Parent Staff Association (PSA). In his Report at Speech Day on 10th December 1947, the Headmaster referred to this, which he hoped would lead to the closer knitting of school and home. It was a body with which staff and governors were associated and which could do much to further the interests of the school. The Association was soon making its mark, as it has done ever since. The June 1948 *Kingstonian* records:

"Several social functions have been held with undoubted success, and on the occasion of the Annual Sports Day, the Association did the catering for a fairly large gathering of boys and parents. At this meeting the Association also provided miniature cups for Senior winners and medals suitably engraved for Junior winners. On July 26th, during the School Cricket Week, the parents are playing the School 1st XI and it is hoped the Association will be able to provide refreshments each day of the week."

At the end of 1947 the pre-war Scientific Society was revived and at the same time the Debating Society and the Gibbon Society seem to have come together, with the latter beginning to hold debates and the former disappearing from sight. Summer term 1948 brought the re-establishment of the Christian Union and the Autumn Term the inaugural meeting of the Photographic Society and of a German Circle to parallel the long-standing activities of the French Circle. The last extra mural body to be formed in Mr James' time was The Griffin Society for social relationships (as the Magazine puts it) between the sixth forms of KGS, Tiffin Boys' and Tiffin Girls'. It started with a bang; a dance, a tennis tournament and a social, all in the summer term, plus a Balloon Debate; but if it survived into the next School

99

year 1949 none of its activities were put on record. So as he retired, sadly to die only two year later, Jimmie James could look back with pride at a School which was certainly in good heart and ready for the leap forward that was to come under his successor who was to take up post in January 1950.

Lovekyn Chantry Lodge

Shortly after the end of the Second World War a group of Old Kingstonians resolved to form a Masonic Lodge composed of Old Boys and Staff of Kingston Grammar School. They enlisted the aid of the Headmaster, and the Second Master, A D Robinson, both of whom were prominent Masons.

In February 1949 the Lovekyn Chantry Lodge was consecrated by the Provincial Grand Master for Surrey. W. Bro. E W H James was installed as the First Worshipful Master, and W. Bro. A D Robinson was appointed Secretary. There were 14 Founder Members of the Lodge.

It was decided that the Lodge should meet four times a year in the School gymnasium and dine in the School Hall. It was no mean task to convert a School gymnasium into a Masonic Temple and in 1949 Masonic furniture was in short supply. Fortunately the Lodge was able to buy furniture from another lodge and the Lodge banner was made by the wife and daughters of Jimmy James (using part of his academic gown for the purpose). That banner is still in use today. The meetings continued to be held in the gymnasium for many years. As the building was unheated it could be very cold in winter for sedentary activities – especially if any windows were broken!

The Government of the School

The radical changes in state education brought about by the 1944 Education Act had little effect on KGS. The Kingston Endowed Schools Trust had been the governing body from 1874 to 1910. Then a new scheme of the Board of Education radically changed the composition of the governing body; the new governors were the Mayor, Aldermen and Burgesses of the Borough of Kingston. The Trust remained as the financial repository of the funds transferred to it in 1874, each year distributing its remaining income, an increasingly insignificant sum, to the three schools, as it was to do right up to 1977, by which time it only covered KGS and Tiffin Boys'. Thus the School was once again directly governed from 1910 onwards as it had been before 1834, by the local authority.

But there was one big difference between its status and that of the two Tiffin schools. They were local authority grammar schools funded and controlled by the local education authority. KGS on the other hand was a Direct Grant grammar school, as were many of the ancient endowed grammar schools throughout the country, regarding themselves as something of an elite. The fact that the Corporation were the governing body through the Kingston Grammar School Committee was incidental. As Cowan (op.cit.) says *"It is thought to be the only Direct Grant School in the country to be governed by a Municipal Authority."*

The Direct Grant status was confirmed by the Minister in October 1945. The Ministry of Education paid an annual capitation grant for every pupil and also made up the difference between the full fee and the amount actually paid in cases where the whole or part of the fees were remitted because parents had a low income. In addition a minimum of 25% of the places in the School were reserved for allocation by the Local Education Authority, Surrey County Council, who paid the fees for those places. Meeting on 9th October 1945 the Kingston Grammar School Committee decided the fees should be set at £30 p.a. and that any parent of a fee-paying pupil should be entitled to a complete remission if the income of the family of two parents and one child did not exceed £7-10-0d per week. A sliding scale for remission applied according to the number of children and the level of parental earnings, so that for example a couple with 4 children would still qualify for a 25% rebate if the parental income did not exceed £12-0-0d per week. This scheme, modified for inflation and for Kingston becoming an Education Authority in its own right, ran on until KGS went independent in 1978.

CHAPTER 10

—··◆··—

The Rundle Years
(1950-1970)

—··◆··—

The New Headmaster – Percy Rundle

THE CHOICE OF A SUCCESSOR TO JIMMIE JAMES was a crucial one. The School had progressed a long way since 1913 when the young Charlie Howse took over a school of less than 100 boys, almost all of whom left by the age of fifteen; a school poorly housed, with no academic record to speak of, and without its own sports field. The only glimmer of light was its hockey record. By 1950 KGS was a school of over 400 boys, had a fair academic record, a substantial range of modern buildings, its own Sports Field at Dinton Road, and the hockey was as good as ever. In short KGS had become an effective local grammar school. But nationally it was by no means in the forefront.

The choice was plain: a consolidator, or someone who would carry the School forward to new achievements. The Kingston Grammar School Committee of the Council which was a mix of Councillors and co-opted members decided to put their faith in a person whose record suggested he would not want to see KGS rest on its laurels. Educated at Plymouth College, Percy Rundle's school record was impeccable, Captain of the 1st XV, member of the 1st XI Cricket, Victor Ludorum at Athletics, he was also CSM in the Cadet Corps. He won an Open Scholarship to King's College, Cambridge in Classics, was a

P W Rundle, Headmaster 1950–70

102

prizeman in Greek verse and Latin prose, and from 1933 to 1940 was 6th Form Classics master at Bury Grammar School. He then served in the Forces till 1946 ending up as Commandant of the 43rd Divisional College BAOR which was the first Army College to be set up in Germany. In 1946 he became Head of Queen Elizabeth Grammar School, Faversham. For the very first time in its history the School had a Headmaster who came with a proven academic and administrative record. The importance of this in the next twenty years as the explosion in higher education, and in the role of the sixth form in secondary schools, took place, could hardly be exaggerated. Percy Rundle knew his way around. And the School was to benefit from this.

In what would now be called a Mission Statement the new Head set out his objectives in the May 1950 issue of the *Kingstonian*. Of tradition he said,

"A lifeless tradition loses all meaning and all worth; it must be constantly refreshed to meet the challenge of changing times. The best and surest way of doing this is for each of you to take all he can from the School – and put back more than he takes, to go hard at everything and do nothing by halves."

He concluded his full page statement with this paragraph:

"We are all of us still in the midst of a struggle and it may be that some day you will have a more vigorous part to play in it than I shall. One side in that struggle knows that conscience is a better master than brute force; the other side thinks that mankind should have no conscience at all. There is no doubt which side we are on. Yet our minds cannot always be dwelling on solemn thoughts of this kind and everyday life is made up of actions done almost without thinking – but conscience can still be at the back of all we do. In the hour before a battle a man's thoughts may well be centred on himself; yet in the prayer which you will often hear in Hall, a courageous man found time before Edgehill to say 'O Lord, Thou knowest how busy I must be this day; If I forget thee, do not Thou forget me'."

Interviewed in 1995, many years after his retirement (he lived until 1998), Percy Rundle said that there were five highlights to the years he spent at the School. These were;

– The very great advance in academic standards over the 21 years.
– His election to the Headmasters' Conference.
– The visit of the Queen on the 400th anniversary of the School's foundation.
– The new Science laboratories at the Fairfield end of the school site.
– The new Sports Field on the Thames opposite Hampton Court.

Academic Standards

In July 1950 eleven boys obtained their Higher School Certificates, with three of them being awarded County Major Scholarships, whilst 37 got their School Certificates. By 1961-62 this was the picture:

- Two Open Scholarships, two State Scholarships, a Guest, Keen and Nettlefold Scholarship, a Rolls Royce Bursary, and a Cadetship to the Royal Navy College, Dartmouth.
- 31 boys were going to University.
- 46 pupils got A levels (equivalent to the old Higher Schools).
- No less than 78 boys gained four or more passes at O Level (equivalent to the old School Certificate).

There is no doubt that with the team of able teachers assembled under him Percy Rundle brought KGS to new levels of academic excellence which have provided the platform on which the even more remarkable achievements of recent years have been based. And it was not because of any dramatic increase in numbers. There were 510 boys in 1950 and no more than 560 in 1970. In a tribute on the Head's retirement the Chairman of the Parent Staff Association, K E Rusby, provided his own summary. In 1950, he said,

"the Sixth Form embraced 60 boys gaining 9 University places .... it now has 160 boys with a record 53 University places including 8 awards to Cambridge, in 1970. This really in one sentence sums up the real achievement of Mr Rundle in his 20 years as Headmaster of KGS. He inherited in 1950 a school which, by our present standards was academically bankrupt. He then proceeded to build a school which now holds it head high as one of the finest educational establishments in the country."

Whilst the last sentence of the tribute may have an element of hyperbole, the figures speak for themselves. As Mr Rusby emphasised, in numbers the School was only 10% larger in 1970 than in 1950, and it had very much the same intake from the locality. Whilst many more children across the country were going on to Higher Education in 1970 than twenty years before, the improvement at KGS far out-stripped average improvements.

Election to the Headmasters' Conference

In 1869 the Reverend Edward Thring, headmaster of Uppingham School, invited the headmasters of 37 of the leading schools in England to meet at his house and form a society of schools which would have an annual conference to discuss educational matters. Twelve headmasters attended that first meeting, but the society gradually grew and was incorporated in 1909. Conferences are still held annually, and membership, limited to 240 Headmasters, has become the generally recognised touchstone for a school to be classed as a Public School, whether boarding or day.

In 1957 Mr Rundle was elected to the Conference, the *Surrey Comet* carrying the headline *"Public School Status for KGS."* In, for him, an unusually immodest statement Mr Rundle said *"Inclusion amongst the Headmasters Conference Schools is a great compliment and not one that is paid lightly."* The

Comet report went on to say that the traditions and history of a school were factors in deciding if it was one which might be elected to the HMC; but also of great importance were its academic standards, the number in the sixth form, exam results and numbers going on to universities.

All the School's subsequent Headmasters have been members of the HMC and the significance of this recognition can hardly be overestimated. It meant, and no doubt means, nothing to the pupils by and large, but it was, for prospective staff and for the parents of prospective pupils, a sign that the School was recognised as in the top flight. Moreover membership could always lapse if the Head and the School fell short of the HMC's exacting standards! So there was an added impetus to strive always to be amongst the best.

The Queen's Visit, 24th March 1961

The School was to celebrate in 1961 the 400th anniversary of its foundation by Queen Elizabeth I. What could be more appropriate than a visit to the School by Queen Elizabeth II? During the summer of 1960 the Chairman of the Governors, Mr K L Kelly, who was also Director-General of the Automobile Association (which no doubt provided some contacts), engaged in discussions with the Palace. On 1st December the Queen's Private Secretary, Sir Michael Adeane, wrote to say that Her Majesty would be pleased to visit the town and the School on 24th March 1961. Much of the next few months was, according to Percy Rundle, spent ensuring that the main purpose of the royal visit, to commemorate the 400th anniversary of the School, was not diminished by the enthusiasm of the town to put the emphasis on the visit to the Borough! Brentwood and Westminster Schools who had recently received royal visits were consulted, the Palace laid down the protocol, and a programme of just under an hour was put together. The School Captain welcomed Her Majesty, there were formal presentations in the Hall, the Headmaster made a speech and the Queen unveiled a commemorative plaque. Processing to the Cage the Queen inspected a detachment of the CCF, the Royal Salute was given, and the National Anthem sung. Moving on to the "Senior School Block" at the Fairfield, the Queen visited the Gymnasium and the new science laboratories, ending her tour at the Library. That was the scene of more presentations and the signing by Her Majesty of a photograph of herself, which now hangs in the School. And then it was over. Responding to a letter of thanks from the Head, Sir Edward Ford, the private secretary who had accompanied the Queen wrote:

"Thank you very much for your letter of 27th March which I have shown to the Queen. Her Majesty was extremely glad to have been able to visit Kingston Grammar School in its Quatercentenary year and is most grateful to you for writing to tell her how much her visit was appreciated by the School. For Her

(*Above*) A Royal Welcome for the Queen from the Juniors
Courtesy *Surrey Comet*

(*Left*) The Queen studies the Charter granted by Elizabeth I
Courtesy *Surrey Comet*

(*Above right*) The Queen inspects a detachment of the Cadet Force
Courtesy *Surrey Comet*

(*Right*) The Queen signs a photograph of herself, for the School.
Courtesy *Surrey Comet*

The signed photograph of Queen Elizabeth II which hangs in the School

Majesty herself the cheers which greeted her announcement of her grant of a week's holiday were eloquent evidence of this."

It was the event itself, the visit to the School by a reigning monarch, that was of the greatest significance, rather than what Her Majesty did on the day. To be one of the handful of schools chosen for a royal visit by the Palace was honour indeed, and the press coverage along with the widely distributed Brochure prepared by the *Surrey Comet, "The Queen Came to Kingston"*, certainly helped to put the School more clearly on the map.

The New Science Laboratories

The laboratories which the Queen saw on her visit in 1961 had in fact been built in 1957, and made possible by the generosity of the Industrial Fund for the Advancement of Scientific Education in Schools. This Fund had been established by contributions from industry, some £3 million in all, to help schools who had to rely on their own resources to have modern laboratories. That KGS needed new plant was not in doubt. The inter-war chemistry and physics labs were far from adequate. The Fund's assessor apparently agreed and the School was offered a grant of £10,500, two thirds of the cost, which was gratefully received.

The new science facilities had no provision for computers; they were so to speak still on the horizon. On 16th July 1962, 19 sixth formers went to Battersea College of Technology to see the workings of an "electronic computer".

The *Kingstonian* of September 1962 recorded:

"At first the group was given a concise lecture on the basis of the computer at the College, 'Sirius', by one of the computer operators, Mr A D Keedwell, an Old Boy of the School. He gave us details of the computers method of performing operations and of how facts are fed into the computer by means of punched tape. In fact, computers are complete idiots, only being able to do what they are told. Telling a computer what to do is called programming. Mr Keedwell completed his lecture by showing how an actual programme could be made up; and the tasks he chose for the computer were to add up all the numbers from 1 to 9,999 and to calculate the factorials up to 30.

The party was then led through a maze of passages and stairways to the Computer Room. The computer itself was unexpectedly small, for although costing £20,000 it consisted of only two five feet tall cabinets about four feet and ten feet long and one foot six inches deep. An idea of the speed of which computers work can be seen from the comment of one of the operators who after the machine had summed all the numbers up to 9,999 in a matter of 2 seconds said "It's running slow today". After a demonstration of more programmes the party was treated to tea and the sight of a second older computer which was being renovated."

A New Sports Field – but not a New School

In 1959 the Governing Body, the Kingston Grammar School Committee of the Council, made a momentous decision. They decided to take a long lease on 22 acres of the Hampton Court Palace Estate to provide a new Sports Ground. The site was, and is, nothing short of magnificent, on the banks of the River Thames, immediately opposite the Palace. But it was low-lying land and thousands of tons of rubble were needed to raise it above the Thames flood level before it could be laid out. The 1961 Appeal Fund was launched to help with the cost of the scheme. The aim was to raise £50,000. An adjoining site on the river bank was bought for a boat house through the generosity of the Boat Club's long time benefactor, R C Sherriff. Ditton Field as it was to be called was finally opened on 1st May 1965. The much smaller and less attractive sports field in North Kingston, at Dinton Road, which had been the

Baldwin of the *Surrey Comet* celebrates the opening of Ditton Field, in May 1965

School's since 1926 was sold. The whole site at Ditton Field was subsequently purchased by the School.

But Percy Rundle's other great dream, that the School itself should be rebuilt on a green field site adjoining the new sports field, was not to be fulfilled. The Governors announced in 1962 that they had acquired an extra three acres next to Ditton Field for this purpose, and subsequently obtained outline planning permission. At Speech Day that year the Chairman said that the response to informal approaches to the Ministry of Education had not been discouraging and indeed gave cause for cautious optimism. The School really had to move, for *"Everybody knows we are desperately cramped for space on the London Road site and I think it must be obvious to any who visit it that it is virtually impossible to extend it."* Although just a couple of years later the Mayor of Kingston was to say when he opened Ditton Field that the School's move would be a good thing in the long run, the tide had already begun to turn against the project. First, Kingston had become a Greater London Borough, incorporating Surbiton and Malden, in what is now called a unitary borough. Surrey County Council had no longer any responsibilities for educating the children of Kingston. Moreover, 1964 saw the change from Conservative to Labour at national level, and the new Government was more concerned to get ahead with its programme of comprehensive schools than to support the building of splendid new direct-grant grammar schools. In effect the plans were put on ice for the duration of the Labour Administration and were brought out again early in the 1970s, when the Heath Government came to power.

A Library Worthy of the Name

In 1866 the mournful entry by the Commissioner for the Endowed Schools Commission was *"Library none"*. Things were not much better in 1924, more than half a century later when the Board of Education Inspectors commented that *"there is no Library properly so called"*. They called for a well furnished library housed in a separate room and properly funded. *"It is understood there is no regular annual grant for the purchase of books. In this matter the School is at a disadvantage as compared with Secondary Schools aided or maintained by the County in which there is an annual library grant of £25"*. Ten years later the Library was getting just £5 a year for books and as late as 1950 still did not have a room of its own.

Small surprise therefore that at the 1958 Inspection the HMIs waxed lyrical at what had at last been achieved. From 1952 the library was housed in the new buildings at the Fairfield, in a fine room which *"provides, besides the bookshelves, accommodation for 22 readers; provision is now being made for 12 more."* The number of books had been doubled from 2000 to 4000 volumes since the new library was opened, and there was a small Junior Library housed elsewhere of 500 books. *"The School is to be congratulated on this record of rapid development. It is the best possible omen for the future .... If the progress of recent years can be maintained it will not be too long before this school has the library which it needs."*

The School Community

"The informal activities of the school show an unusually high degree of vitality and for this much credit is attributable to senior boys, who show initiative and enthusiasm in running clubs and societies, and of course to the masters who help them." This comment by the Inspectors in 1958 certainly holds good for any and every generation at KGS over the following 40 years. But school societies are for the most part like rivers flowing through limestone rock, they appear and when the initial enthusiasm dies away, disappear from sight, sometimes for ever, sometimes to reappear a schoolboy generation or two later. And that is as it should be, for nothing could be worse than for all the societies to become institutions. Thus in 1958 there was the CCF, the Gibbon Society, the French Circle, the Spanish Circle, the Christian Union, the Heraldry Society, the Geological Society, the Railway Society, and the Stamp Club, plus a Junior Debating Society, all providing reports on their activities for the *Kingstonian*. By 1970 the picture had changed. Now we read in the *Kingstonian* of the KGS Press, the Football Society, the Radio Astronomy Society, and a (reborn) Scientific Society. A Transport Society had been formed, not to be confused with the Railway Enthusiasts' Society. Heraldry, geology, stamp collecting and the two foreign language circles had disappeared, at least for the time being, from the pages of the School Magazine.

The three activities which were there in 1958 and 1970, indeed with a record stretching back before the 20th century in the case of the Gibbon Society, to the First World War in the case of the CCF and to the 1930s for the Christian Union, all had the advantage of attracting a widespread audience. The military, argumentation, and religion cover a lot of schoolboy interests! Each of the three has a clearly defined objective and all have benefited from active adult participation whether in the foreground, with the CCF, or in the background with the Gibbon Society and the CU. What is more each offered, and still does, what the clientele wanted. Thus in 1970 the Gibbon Society, as well as debates, was organising trips to the West End theatres. The RAF Section of the CCF was involved in preparing the Hut for the arrival of a Link Trainer, and whilst numbers going to the CCF Annual Camp were down, the Christian Union was taking 70 on their annual summer camp in Devon.

Of course school societies form only part of the extra mural activities. As well as sport (see Chapter 15), the destinations for school journeys read like a Baedeker of European cities. South of France, San Sebastian, Paris, Easter in Italy, Tours, Madrid, St Malo, ski-ing at Saas-Fee, a Rhine Cruise, a trip to Leningrad and Moscow (in 1965 and 1968), Venice, Copenhagen, Innsbruck, and Rome all figure during the Rundle years. And the range of what might broadly be called "cultural activities" was steadily expanded. Drama began to be taken more seriously. Christmas Entertainments were still the order of the day in the early 50s, with dramatised extracts from *Alice in Wonderland* in 1953, *The Dyspeptic Ogre* and *Androcles and the Lion* in 1954, and three one-act humorous plays in 1956. With the development of Junior House plays (scoring points towards the House Championship) interest in drama certainly grew; school plays became much more ambitious. 1965 saw Anouilh's *Becket*, 1966 Shakespeare's *Henry IV* and 1967 Shaw's *The Devil's Disciple*; and the same year a Drama Studio for the English Department took over the Lovekyn Chapel from the Junior Library. Mr Rundle went out to the strains of Joan Littlewood's *Oh, What a Lovely War*, an ambitious musical production, involving members of local girls' schools in the cast. There were even staff plays during this period in the late 50s including *Arsenic and Old Lace*.

It cannot be said that the musical side of the School's life progressed at the same pace. Most of the time there was a school choir and a school orchestra but, one or two outstanding individuals apart, they did not scale any great musical heights. The fact that there was no Music Room did not help. The Inspectors' Report in 1958 said that part of the trouble was that there was not a music course up to GCE and A levels. *"Boys who wish to offer music for external examinations are coached privately."* There were, the Inspectors reported, only 36 books in the music section of the Library. None of the singing heard at the Inspection *"reached a high level and at times it lacked vitality and finish."* It was, the Inspector said, *"disappointing to find that the former strong interest in instrumental work has all but vanished"*. All this is not to say that there was an absence of music-making. A voluntary choir took part in the Carol Service, and there was an annual Concert at which some serious music was played. In 1965 for instance the resurrected School Orchestra played Mozart's Symphony No 36 (The Linz) and Wagner's Prelude to Act III of Lohengrin; at the same concert there was a madrigal group, a choir, and several soloists.

The Red and Grey

For many years right up to the end of the 1980's the Editors of the *Kingstonian* regarded the school magazine as a journal of record, and little else. Budding writers found no place in its pages. Undeterred they produced their own unofficial magazines. First there was the *Red and Grey* which flourished between 1950 and 1960. Edited by a panel of sixth formers, who were the main contributors, the *Red and Grey* appeared each term in its heyday. One of those Editors, who was to achieve literary fame in adult life, cut his teeth with articles in the magazine. They showed the catholicity of approach evident in his later work, A View of Luxembourg, The River in Winter at Kingston, Ordinary People, The Kingston Cine Club, and short stories, The

Journey, The Long Day's Waiting and Escape in the Morning. His name was Michael Frayn (see p. 115). Junior members of the School did not get much of a look-in, but J. Belcher's poem in the November 1953 edition brought an unstuffy approach to his subject:

EXAMS

Again we sit in blank despair
And pass our fingers through our hair.
Number one's a puzzle indeed;
We try it now with utmost speed.
We sit there, wondering how to do
The second part of number two.
Number three is even worse than those -
We sit and twiddle thumbs and toes.
And number four – oh, help us do! -
It's worse by far than number two.
At number five we groan again,
And even looking gives us a pain.
Oh help! Oh help! There's still ten more;
We sit and idly watch the door.
The bell then goes, we shout hurray!
Exams are over for today.

The existence of the *Red and Grey*'s successor, *The Contemporary* is recorded from 1964 to 1967 by which time it was a very serious-minded endeavour. "Britain and the World Food Crisis" was the theme and the magazine was expected to *"enjoy a wide distribution throughout the student body of the country"* (*Kingstonian*, 1967). The same year saw *Kingston Writes*, a student outlet for the imaginative writing of boys in the School. Nothing if not ambitious the Editors sent their volume to David Holbrook, well known English don at King's Cambridge, who said he had read the collection with great interest and was *"amazed by the strength and variety of emotion displayed."*

The Old Kingstonian Association

Any association of former pupils exists for three reasons, to keep in touch with the School, to keep in touch with each other, and to a much lesser extent to share common interests. For Old Boys in this period the first two aims were met by the distribution to every member of the Old Kingstonian Association of each edition of the school magazine; and, of course the Annual Dinner, often held in the School Hall. Other social activity, the third aim, varied as it always had, according to the interests of the Old Boys activists, that small core of enthusiasts without which the Association would have expired. So, in 1951 the OK Dramatic Club produced a play called *Easy Money* and in 1953 *Pink*

String and Sealing Wax. The annual Dance at the Griffin Hotel drew 60 couples in 1953. In 1954 there was a "Soiree Afloat" on the Thames, and the Golf Section was restarted (it carries on to this day). A car rally in the form of a treasure hunt took place in the summer of 1957.

A continuing problem, however, for the OKA was membership. Despite the efforts of successive Committees the number of members never bore any resemblance to the number of former pupils. In 1958 the Committee were congratulating themselves on passing the 400 mark, and in fact there was no significant increase on this till some 20 years later, when all leavers were automatically enrolled as members from the time they left school. Meantime an innovation was to have an annual Old Boys' Day at Ditton Field. Starting in 1966 with two cricket matches against the School, tennis matches were included in later years. One ever present feature of the event has been a licensed marquee, or Beer Tent as the younger participants prefer to call it!

In 1967 the OKA and the Old Kingstonian Hockey Club, which had always led independent lives, decided to merge. This was a very brave attempt to build strength through the various interests, but it had only limited success perhaps because whilst the hockey players had one clear interest, hockey, the rest of the Association had a wide range of interests. But overall the period was one of strength and on 11th July 1970 there were over 150 people present after tea on Open Day at Ditton Field to make a presentation to the retiring Headmaster. The fact that one of the books presented to Mr Rundle was entitled *Early Greek Maidens* caused some amusement, particularly as the main gift was a powerful set of binoculars.

Michael Frayn – Author and Dramatist

One Old Kingstonian, at the beginning of his time in the sixth form when Percy Rundle took over in 1950, had by the time of the Head's retirement presentation already become a nationally acclaimed author and playwright. In 1951-2 Michael Frayn won the Humphrey Memorial Prize for English, and a State Scholarship to Emmanuel College, Cambridge. Reporter and Columnist on the *Guardian* (1957-62) and then on the *Observer* (1962-8) he won the Hawthornden Prize in 1966 for his book *The Russian Interpreter*. His career has continued with an array of plays and books including several that have gained critics awards – *Alphabetical Order, Donkeys Years, Noises Off, Benefactors* and *Copenhagen.* His novel, *Headlong*, was shortlisted for the Booker Prize in 1999. He has always remained a good friend of the School and of the OKA.

Albert Perry – Art Master

An individual who might well have appeared in a comedy of Michael Frayn's (but did not) and who simply cannot be omitted from the story of the School is Albert Perry who was visiting art master from 1919 to 1953. Because it is impossible to do justice to all the contributions of the many outstanding members of staff over the years, and to select just a handful would seem invidious, potted biographies are outside the scope of this book. But every rule has its exception. An extract from the *Kingstonian* of September 1953 gives the feel of the most extraordinary "character" ever to teach at KGS:

"More than one national newspaper has a file stuffed with press cuttings about him. He is well known for his Bohemian style of dress and the vividly coloured envelopes which he sends through the post. Pulling the leg of The Royal Academy has been his chief hobby and many are the exploits in which he has indulged. He has often displayed his paintings in unexpected places including a costermongers cart, a Thames barge towed up the river from Richmond, and more recently a Tooting hostelry."

"He is known far and wide as "the worlds most rejected artist", a self-description as misleading as some of his self-portraits. In fact, the Société Nationale des Beaux Arts and the Société des Artistes Français regularly show his work, as do the Royal Institute of Oil Painters, the Scottish Academy, and The Royal College of Art .... The boys at the end of term showed their appreciation of Tecky, as they called himfor years, by presenting him with a cheque. 'The boys' to quote the Headmaster's words 'think tremendously of him' (quiff and all)."

Conclusion

Although it was written in 1958 by Her Majesty's Inspectors, at the end of a four day inspection, their summary of what they had found could well have been written in 1970 when Percy Rundle retired:

"The remarkable growth in numbers has been accompanied by an equally remarkable growth in the extent and quality of the work at the top of the school. The new buildings have added much to the schools amenities and educational scope. Recent achievement is admirable; future possibilities seem full of promise. The boys have a wide variety of talents. If the school does not relax its efforts to evaluate these talents accurately and develop them even more effectively, there is every reason to hope that this ancient and vigorous foundation will reach new heights of success."

—··◆··—

CHAPTER 11

Both Independent and Co-Ed
(1970-1991)

—··◆··——··◆··—

T
HREE HEADMASTERS SPANNED the life of the School during the
1970s and 1980s. First came John Strover, then Sidney Miller and
finally Tony Creber. Between them they saw the School through a
particularly turbulent period. All of them came to KGS with much teaching
experience. John Strover had a Mathematics degree from Oxford (Trinity
College) and had captained the University Hockey side. After three years at
Canford School he went to Harrow where he taught Mathematics,
Economics, and Divinity, becoming the School's Careers Master in 1960. He
joined KGS in 1970, remaining as Head till 1977 when he moved on to
became head of Warwick School. His successor, Sidney Miller had graduated
from Cambridge with a First in Classics and after three years at Clifton went
to Eton to teach Classics, becoming Head of Department in 1971. In 1974 he
took the unusual step of moving to be Deputy Head of a Comprehensive
School, Bridgewater Hill, at Milton Keynes and was still only 34 when he
became Headmaster at KGS in 1977. He was to stay nine years before
moving on to be Head of Bedford School. In January 1987 Tony Creber took
over, after a one term interregnum when the Deputy Head Gordon Evans, to
everyone's delight took over the Headmaster's role; he had been on the staff
since 1950 and was an Old Boy (1935-44). Tony's background was rather
different from his predecessors. A graduate of London University he came
from Hampton School where he had been Deputy Head. After an action-
packed four and a half years he decided to retire, in July 1991.

A New School – Why not?

1970 not only saw a change of Headmaster, it saw a change of Government.
Out went the Harold Wilson Administration. In came the Ted Heath
Government. Now, at the centre, there were Ministers who valued the
Grammar School and Public School ethos in a way that a Labour

John Strover, Headmaster 1970–1977

(*Right*) The Planned New School at Ditton Field 1972

Administration never would. It was time to take up the cudgels again. A brand new school adjoining the superb playing fields on the Thames directly opposite to Hampton Court Palace began again to look a real possibility. There followed five years of increasing frustration. Reading the minutes of the Kingston Grammar School Committee of Kingston Council (who were still the Governing Body) it seemed that no sooner was one hurdle cleared than another had to be jumped.

The first hurdle was the composition of the Committee itself. It consisted of eleven members of Kingston Council, two from Surrey County Council, and just six non-Council members. Though most (or even all) the 13 Councillors may have been persuaded of the merits of the move of the School to Ditton Field, it was clearly going to be left to the six to drive the project forward. It would not be unreasonable to assume that, in fact, quite a few of the 13 Councillors would at best have been lukewarm supporters. For what was in it for Kingston? It was going to lose its ancient Grammar School, relocated well beyond the Borough Boundary to a fairly inaccessible part of Surrey (and Kingston was by now entirely independent of Surrey for all purposes). The new school was certainly not as convenient at Ditton Field as at London Road for many of its in-Borough pupils. In short, what was by 1970 as much a gem in the Borough's educational crown as the Tiffin Schools, was going to disappear.

Despite the Head's determination and valiant efforts by some Governors the general impression is of a committee dogged by hesitancy and delay. For

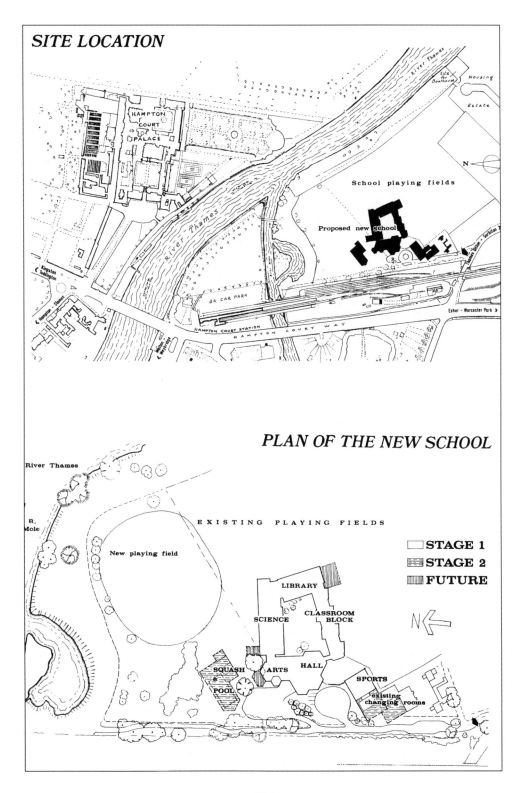

SITE LOCATION

PLAN OF THE NEW SCHOOL

instance, in January 1971 the Department of Education and Science, with whom everything had to be cleared because of the direct grant status, asked what was happening about an Appeal for funding the new school. It was due to be launched on 17 November, but finally got off the ground a full 18 months later (with a change of the firm conducting the campaign en route), in April 1973. Next there was the fact that the DES themselves admitted they were not at all sure how to handle the financial side of the move to Ditton Field. They were sure that the costs were too high, but admitted they had seldom dealt with a direct grant school that was building on a new site, from scratch; they played it along very carefully indeed. The Governors were told, in 1973, that the building costs were considered to be 10% to 20% too high, and that their plan would provide 30% more space than the Department would regard as necessary for a Maintained Grammar School. Back to the drawing board, and in succession two, more modest, designs for the new school building were produced. Now at last the DES gave their approval. An overall cost of £1,108,000 was to be the limit, to be provided from three sources: the sale of the London Road buildings (£542,000), the Appeal, just launched (£88,000) and the rest by loan, to be repaid out of the School Revenue account (i.e. from pupils' fees).

There was a minatory note though. The minutes record that the Department stressed the point about the impact of rising cost, and the Governors were recommended to proceed as quickly as possible to the tender stage. But it was not that easy. There had been difficulties over the use of the London Road site; should it be entirely residential or include offices on the London Road frontage? Questions were raised about access. There had to be a public enquiry, and to cap it all a Kingston Councillor who did not favour the move got the Victorian range of buildings spot listed as of historic interest. To get them de-listed required another public enquiry, and more legal expense. It was not until January 1975 that all the clearances were given, including permission to pull down the School's Listed Victorian buildings.

But by then it was too late. Labour were back in power nationally, and there was burgeoning inflation. The agreed costs were by now nowhere near what was needed and a plea to the DES to raise the limit was rejected on 11th September 1974. The plan for a new school was dead in the water, to be thought of as just a "might have been".

There were probably as many sighs of relief as there were of disappointment. Certainly had the building work started in 1975 there would have been a big chance that an inadequate, truncated school would have resulted, as cut after design cut was made to keep within the DES budget – a rather poor building on a lovely site. But would it in any case have been the right site for a town Grammar School? There were always people who thought not. The drawbacks of the London Road site were obvious. It was cramped. Parking was difficult. There was not space to expand beyond around 600 pupils, so

Artist's impressions of the planned New School

(*top*) View from the River Thames
(*bottom*) Assembly Hall from Courtyard

KGS could never become a big school. Playground space was at a premium. It was on a very busy road. But, on the other hand, it was at the heart of the local transport system, and in a regional shopping centre, a town bustling with life. And it was Kingston's school in a way it never would be at Ditton. In any event the fact the School had to stay in Kingston turned out to be no disaster academically. Neither at the time nor at any period since has the School found difficulty in attracting first rate staff or an ample intake of children of high potential.

Finally, the one undeniable result of chasing what turned out to be a will o' the wisp for so many years was that the School lost more than a decade of good building time. From 1960 to 1974 sights were set on the new school. It would have made no sense to build anything substantial at London Road. The building boom in the earlier part of Percy Rundle's time at KGS ceased, and it was not until 1975, after the thumbs down from the DES that ambitious building plans were put forward to the Governors, by John Strover. His plans for a major extension at the Fairfield end were repeatedly blocked by the Committee, not on merit, nor even on costs, for the money from the new school Appeal would have helped. Rather the Councillors knew that their time was drawing to a close. Perhaps they did not want to get involved in further plans for additional school buildings? For KGS was about to become an independent school right outside the State system. They simply agreed to huts being erected on the north side of the Cage!

Going Independent

In 1975 the Labour Government faced the direct grant grammar schools of the country with a stark choice. Go independent and become financially self-supporting, or be fully integrated into the maintained system. KGS was one of over 100 of the old endowed grammar schools who made up the bulk of the direct grant sector, and had no hesitation in deciding for independence. In March 1975 the Kingston Grammar School Committee voted unanimously for this move. The change of status would mean a new Governing Body, the withdrawal of free places sponsored by local education authorities and also the direct grant subsidy of fees by the Government. In addition there was, of course, the removal of the sense of security which came from being associated with the state education system. It would be for the school to decide on the level of fees; they would have to be set high enough to cover costs, and to permit a number of scholarships and bursaries to be awarded.

This was going to mean considerable change and one of the biggest concerns was that academic standards might drop because of the need to trawl lower down the ability range to fill the School with fee-paying pupils. For by 1973 half the entry was of boys with free places awarded on the results of competitive examination, the fees met by the local authorities (30 each year from Kingston, 14 from Surrey and 5 from Sutton.) When independent it was expected there would simply be 7 Governors' Scholarships (split between full remission of fees and half remission) with another seven means tested bursaries of varying amounts. John Strover summarised the effects on the School in a note for parents (reproduced in the autumn 1975 issue of the *Kingstonian*):

"It is the Governors' wish to preserve the high academic standards of the School and, as far as possible its social mix and they have decided that they can only do this by becoming fully independent of the State system. This means in effect that parents of boys entering the School from September 1976 onwards will have to pay full fees .... though boys who have been admitted to the School before the end of the current academic year will attract the Direct Grant during the remainder of their school career.

.... We shall be seeing several changes in our intake over the next few years. Principal among these will be the formation of a preparatory form (discontinued in 1965 and now reintroduced) starting next September into which will be admitted 30 boys at 10+. Places in the prep form will be competed for by examination, to be held in the Spring term and those who are successful will be assured a place in the main school and may also compete for Scholarships/Bursaries at 11+ and 13+. The entry at 11+ will be reduced to 60 boys next September and from 1978 the entry at 13+ will be increased to 24 boys. The size of the School will not be substantially altered and when these changes have finally worked through it is expected that there will be about 550 boys in the School."

The Endowed Schools Trust – Distribution of Funds

What then was to be done with the remainder of the capital still held by the Kingston Endowed Schools Trust and still bringing in a few hundred pounds a year, most of the trust funds having been spent many years before on building KGS and the two Tiffin Schools? These funds had been put into the trust from the endowments of KGS, the whole of the Tiffin Charity, and the assets of nine other local educational charities in 1874. It was decided they should be divided between Tiffin Boys' and KGS equally (Tiffin Girls' School had opted out in 1940). The details are set out in the Charity Commissioners' 1978 Scheme of Government under which, with minor amendments, the School still operates. KGS was to get £63,000 of investments, and properties, valued at the time at just £3500, with similar sums to Tiffins. There were some oddities! The School became entitled to a fee-farm rent of 60p *"issuing out of property now in the possession or ownership of Bentalls"*. Similarly £2.24 was due each year from the Council for Eagle Wharf, £1 from the Angel Inn on the Portsmouth Road, £1.50 for the Bittoms, £1 for 21 Church Street, and £1.50 for 31 Market Place. More mysteriously the Commissioners in 1978 awarded the School a fee-farm rent of £21.78 a year for land *"at Lechlade Manor now in the possession or ownership*

123

of the Sisterhood of Clothilde" and another of £7.20 for land at *"Blaisdon Manor, now in the possession or ownership of the Salesian School"*. Perhaps they should be collected, especially the 60p a year from Bentalls!

One piece of land was of rather more importance, the Fairfield.

The School and the Fairfield

The Fairfield is a large, enclosed Recreation Ground, in the heart of Kingston. It lies immediately to the south of the Public Library, the Kingston Kingfisher Centre and, at its eastern end, the main buildings of the School. It is the site of the Borough's May Merrie and the August Children's Fun Day; the Circus and Fun Fair come there, and its football and cricket pitches are in regular use. The Fairfield is a major civic amenity. It was not always so. In his book *Half a Century of Kingston History* published in 1887, F S Merryweather looks back to the beginning of Queen Victoria's reign and writes:

"It was an untidy and unenclosed waste, on which the roughs of Water Lane were prone to indulge too freely in horseplay and across which at night, it was dangerous to pass. Its deplorable condition was brought to the notice of the Town Council as early as 1848, but its members refused even to discuss the subject of its improvement until 1859." (p. 17.)

This is where the School entered the picture, for a considerable part of the land that made up the Fairfield was theirs. There could be no public, enclosed, Recreation Ground unless the School sold or leased its land to the Council. In 1864 an 80 year lease was agreed at an annual rent of £65, which was certainly no peppercorn sum at the time. Unfortunately there was no provision for rent review! The description, in the 1874 Schedule of real estate to be transferred to the new Kingston Endowed Schools' Trust, is of four separate pieces of land, three of one acre each and the other of two rods.

So now the freehold of the School's Fairfield land, as all its endowments, passed to the new governing Trust. That Trust was empowered to use its capital to build and improve the three Schools for which it was to have responsibility, KGS, Tiffin Boys' and Tiffin Girls'. At various times various assets were therefore sold and this included the sale to the Council of some of the leased land, in 1912. But the Endowed Schools Trust still held on to the freehold of a part, and presumably continued to receive the appropriate part of the original £65 a year rent. In 1944, when all this was dim and distant history, the total income of the Trust almost insignificant anyway, and with both Tiffin and KGS under governance by the local authority, the 80 year lease ended. A new lease of the Trust's freehold land should have been negotiated by the Trustees, but it was not. No one apparently noticed. Certainly no one took any action. And yet this freehold land was of real value. It may well have been that, if anyone did look at the matter in 1944, they concluded one might as well let sleeping dogs lie.

Masters v Boys Football Match 1976
The boys won 8 –1 thanks to their "stylish" tackling

Whatever the reason, sleeping dogs did lie for another 33 years until the Trust had to be wound up! There then came to light three strips of land, some three and half acres still in the freehold of the Trust. In the 1978 scheme which the Commissioners prepared, two strips of land at the eastern end of the Fairfield were awarded to Tiffin Boys', and a strip at the Western end to the School. This is described as:

"Land containing 40,800 square feet or thereabouts having frontage on the north to Fairfield Road, on the south to Fairfield South and on the west to Fairfield West being the western part of the Fairfield." (Scheme 398(S) 78. Second Schedule 5(3)).

The western part of the Fairfield is the main entrance into the grounds. The Council expressed interest in purchasing all three strips from the two Schools both in 1977 and again in the 1990s, but at the time this history draws to a close in 1999 substantive negotiations were still underway to resolve the long standing impasse. One thing was clear to both Schools' Governors; they did not plan to surrender the title to their part of the Fairfield!

The Fairfield story is an interesting example of how the close links between School and Borough could result in a confusion of interests. If School and Borough had been less intertwined the terms of the 1864 lease might have been different; and there might not have been 33 years of inaction when the lease expired in 1944. As it was, by 1949 the Council's own Property

Committee were the Controlling Committee of the Endowed Schools' Trust Land, and were taking decisions whether or not to dispose of particular properties (Committee Minutes 9th June 1949). The Town Clerk was their Secretary; he was also clerk to the Council's Kingston Grammar School Committee.

The Governing Body of the School

With independence came a new governing body, very different from the Council's Kingston Grammar School Committee. The detail is set out in the Charity Commissioners' 1978 Scheme. In place of 13 Councillors and six co-opted members the new body was to have nine nominative and nine co-optive governors. The nominees were to be as follows:

> one each from
> Kingston Council
> Surrey County Council (withdrew in 1996)
> Cambridge University
> London University
> Kingston Polytechnic (later Kingston University)
> Kingston Council of Churches;
> two from the Old Kingstonian Association; and
> one from the Parents' and Staff Association, "*not
> being a parent guardian or person having the
> actual custody of a pupil attending the School.*"

The nine co-opted governors come from a wide range of professions, folk who have had relevant skills to offer, accountants, lawyers, financiers, doctors, journalists. Gone was the Town Clerk as Clerk to the Governors. That role was taken over by the Bursar, first appointed in September 1976, and an essential full time member of staff once the School was entirely responsible for its financial integrity.

There has been only one significant change in the 1978 scheme; it had to be amended to allow for girls to become pupils.

Going Co-educational

It is a nice question whether or not KGS would have become a mixed school if the direct grant system had continued. The idea was certainly never given serious consideration before the decision to go independent was taken, but once the substantial and assured income which the direct grant system brought to the school had ceased, the possibility had to be considered. The fees were not going to be low. For 1977-78 they were set at £822 per annum. Were there enough parents of able boys willing to pay this, remembering of course that the two Tiffin Schools were still providing a first rate free grammar school education in the Borough and that a number of other

Sidney Miller, Headmaster 1977–88

Secondary Schools, like Tolworth Girls' and Coombe Girls', had built up sound academic reputations? On the other hand there was no major independent school in the area that was co-educational so that tactically there was an opening, and one which KGS seized with alacrity. In 1977-78 the old and new governing bodies were operating in tandem for a transitional year. Both saw the merit of opening the doors to girls and Sidney Miller, the new Head, held a press conference on 17th November to announce that from September 1978 girls would be allowed to join the sixth form; in September 1979 girls would be admitted at 10, 11 and 13 on the same terms as boys. There was some protest from the Old Kingstonians, mainly that they had not been consulted. Comment from a third former recorded in the *Borough News* was more positive. *"I suppose it will brighten things up a bit"* said Mark Appleton, *"Having girls there will give us the incentive to work harder. I wouldn't like a girl to be doing better than me."* An anonymous sixth former said *"As Tiffin is closing down as a grammar school they will need somewhere for the girls to go"*, a rather skewed view of comprehensive education as pursued by the Government. In fact Kingston never put forward any plans for comprehensive schools in the Borough and both Tiffin Schools survived unscathed.

September 1978 saw the first nine girls enter the sixth form and the next

Tony Creber, Headmaster
1988–91

autumn brought the first intake at the bottom of the School. It was one of Sidney Miller's principal achievements that he oversaw the smooth transition of KGS from being a boys' grammar school to a co-ed establishment and without any drop over an eight year period in either academic or sporting standards. By 1987 numbers had settled at about 60% boys and 40% girls though they were later to come a little closer to equality. It certainly has been remarkable that with a cadre of only 300–350 boys in place of 550 before going co-ed, school teams on the hockey field and on the river have scaled heights never achieved before. Similarly with only 200–250 girls, the Kingstonian for 1991 records eight girls playing for Surrey elevens and the first Blue for hockey, Jane Reid. As for the rowing, the comment in the same edition of the magazine that the whole of the girls 1st VIII was selected for some form of International Team speaks for itself, *"This must be some record in itself, by any school or club in the country."* (See Chapter 15 which details modern sporting achievements.) It was of course going to take rather longer to achieve a balanced staffroom, but by the time Tony Creber arrived the move was in that direction. Of 48 staff, nine were women and 39 men.

The Assisted Places Scheme

In 1977 it looked as though the School would have to paddle its own canoe, so far as finances were concerned; having gone independent there would be just a handful of bursaries and scholarships. Perhaps 80% of all children entering the school would have to pay full fees. But Labour was defeated in the 1979 General Election, and a more sympathetic Conservative Administration took over. They could not put the clock back; the direct grant grammar schools were gone for ever but they did the next best thing by bringing in the Assisted Places Scheme. Under this, fee-paying schools like KGS could apply for a number of assisted places. KGS went for 24 each year on entry. What this amounted to was a national bursary scheme – the Ministry paid the fees entirely for poor families and made partial payment on a sliding scale up to what might be termed lower middle income families. The scheme had weaknesses but it did mean that the social mix, always a feature of a good grammar school, could continue. In 1997 the new Labour Government immediately after the General Election abolished the scheme, though of course permitting those with assisted places already at the School to retain them. So 20 years on the School faced the same sort of situation on fees as it had in 1977. But it was in a much stronger position, with 20 years as a co-ed public school, an academic and sporting reputation which was unrivalled, and buildings which were perhaps for the first time ever almost adequate to the needs of an expanding curriculum.

The New Buildings

John Strover had his plans for extension to the Fairfield block repeatedly deferred, and finally turned down by the old Kingston Grammar School Committee in 1975 and 1976. The new Governing body was more sympathetic and the new Head, Sidney Miller, was able to report that four rooms in the "Lovekyn Chapel Annexe", the cottage adjoining the Chapel, had been decorated and furnished as Music Practice rooms, cloakroom facilities, rest room and showers provided for girls in the Junior Building, all completed in 1979, whilst 1980 would see an additional storey on the main Fairfield building. A senior Modern Languages room, a senior Maths room, a seminar room, a careers suite and a new sixth form Common Room would be provided. Much of the money was to come from the Appeal of 1974 "Another Way Ahead" which absorbed the aborted "New School" Appeal.

The third Appeal in the School's post-war history was launched in 1982, the results of which exceeded the most optimistic forecasts. Prefabricated huts in the Fairfield Quadrangle were replaced by two science labs, a Computer Centre and an additional classroom. The Junior Library got a home in a new prefab which completed the row of such buildings alongside the Cage; and perhaps of most note to every Old Kingstonian, the block of outdoor lavatories adjoining the Cadet Force building was at last knocked down.

More was to come with the launch of a further Appeal in 1988 to create a multi-purpose Lecture Theatre, and a study area, with a new Library above, on the site of the old mini bus shed (at an earlier time the cycle shed), and to replace the huts by the Cage with a new building for Art, and Design and Technology. Tony Creber gave much of his energy and time to forwarding this project which was largely completed before he left in the summer of 1991. The Appeal was by far the most successful ever undertaken, raising £475,000. One major donation by an Old Kingstonian, Derek Finlay, made it possible to add another feature, an Art Gallery running the length of the South side of the Junior Building, adjoining the Art and Technology building. It was named after the donor, the Finlay Gallery. Taken together these new buildings were the most exciting architecture KGS had ever seen. Of the Library it could fairly be said that the School, which proceeded to employ a professional librarian, had a facility of which any school in the land could be proud. There would be more extensions to the School plant in the 1990s.

Whilst all this work may indeed have indicated the truth of the saying that necessity is the mother of invention it makes clear that the view in the 60s that the School must move if it was to keep pace with the space demands of a modern curriculum were really not justified.

Academic Achievement

In 1970 KGS was a boys' grammar school producing very good sixth form results. By 1990 it was a co-ed grammar school producing quite excellent results. The school remained much the same size throughout the 20 years. In summer 1990, 69 sixth formers gained A Levels, and there were 47 subject passes that were A Grade. The overall calibre of teaching can be seen from the wide range of subjects in which these A grades were obtained, Biology, Chemistry, French, Geography, History, Mathematics, Further Mathematics, Economics, Physics, and Art. Meanwhile at GCSE level 89 pupils gained passes in four or more subjects and no less than 14 of these got at least eight straight A grades. Practically every sixth former leaving that summer, 63 in all, was going on to university.

One remarkable feature of the Advanced Level grade A passes was that 18 of them, well over a third, were in Mathematics and Further Mathematics. This was indicative of the strength of teaching in this area, built up over many years by the team of which Hans Woyda was the outstanding leader. A brilliant mathematician, an extraordinarily talented teacher of his subject, he died suddenly, aged only 53, in 1981 after 31 years at the School. In his memory the H G Woyda Trust was established with Memorial Mathematics prizes and a Travel Bursary.

Music and Drama

In 1970-71 musical activity was still in a minor key, the provision of musical backing for a production of *The Hollow Crown* being the only activity mentioned in the *Kingstonian* for that year. By Tony Creber's last year, 1990-91, a confident Music Department, now with three staff, and backed by a

Michael Frayn, an Old Kingstonian, acclaimed author and playwright comes to judge the Junior Drama Competition in 1984 – Courtesy *Surrey Comet*

Music Society open to friends and to parents as well as pupils, undertook its second continental journey, to Bad Walsee. Hosted by the Bad Walsee Gymnasium they performed two concerts. Back in Kingston, the orchestra performed Haydn's London Symphony, and Corelli's Christmas Concerto as part of their repertoire. Chamber music, with both Senior and Intermediate Wind Ensembles and a Chamber Choir were flourishing. At an informal level the Music Society presented a Trad Jazz Concert and a concert of Baroque Music during the year, and raised £1000 to subsidise the trip to Germany.

As to the reasons for the great strides which took place in these two decades, the first has to be the interest shown by successive Headmasters who were either musicians or at least appreciative of good music. Tony Creber founded a Music prize to go to the musician who contributed most to school music over the year. The strengthening of the teaching staff in the Music Department widened opportunities and the introduction from 1978 onwards of Governors' Music Scholarships meant that by the mid 1980s there was a strong cadre of talented young musicians right through the School. And as well as the Music Society, the contribution of the KGS Choral Society must not be overlooked. Formed in 1981 this was, and still is, the vehicle for an annual Oratorio Concert; pupils, parents and friends combining under the Baton of the Senior Music Master.

School Drama was already strong when Percy Rundle left in 1970. It

A scene from Alan Ayckbourn's play *A Chorus of Disapproval*, the Senior production in 1989

continued to be so. The 70s saw, for instance productions of Shaw's *Major Barbara*, Oliver Goldsmith's *She Stoops to Conquer*, Shakespeare's *The Tempest* and Tom Stoppard's *The Real Inspector Hound*, in tandem with Peter Shaffer's *Black Comedy*. In the 80s came equally ambitious productions: *Measure for Measure*, Ayckbourn's *A Chorus of Disapproval*, Pinter and more Stoppard, Terence Rattigan's *French Without Tears*, *Twelfth Night*, and in 1990 John Mortimer's *A Voyage Round My Father*. Senior performances continued to be backed up by the annual Junior Drama Competition, where many KGS young actors started their careers.

But there was one event which outshone all others. That was the production of the original KGS Musical *Smike* in March 1973. To quote from the *Kingstonian*, autumn 1973:

"This musical adaptation of Nicholas Nickleby, with music and words written largely by Mr Simon May and Mr Clive Barnett was rapturously applauded by capacity audiences at each of the four performances given at the Surbiton Assembly Rooms. The operetta attracted wide critical acclaim and the LP album of the music from the show was rapidly sold out."

Performed all over the English speaking world since then, the operetta, with a professional cast, formed part of the BBC's Christmas entertainment that year. As for its producer and musical director, Simon May, he was soon to leave teaching for a career on the national stage as a well known writer and performer of popular music, incidental music for TV and films, with many stints as a DJ thrown in.

The Kingstonian

A dramatic event of a very different kind took place in 1989. For 106 years, since its very first edition, the school magazine, first as the *Annual Register* and then as the *Kingstonian* had been a journal of record. Exam results, sports results and school activities, not to mention biographies of departing masters and accounts of the annual prize-giving, these were its very lifeblood. In 106 years just about the only thing that changed in the School magazine was the cover design, four times, the introduction of largely formal photographs and, for a few recklessly adventurous years (1965-1980), the inclusion of some very sober advertising, by banks, the Armed forces and the like. Autumn 1988 gave no hint of what was to come. Its 44 close printed pages with pictures in it of the Head with the prefects, the boys and girls 1st Elevens, Hockey, and the 1st Eleven Cricket along with one of *"Medallists at the National Rowing Championships and Winners of Junior Victrix Ludorum"* was par for the course. So was the diagonal red and white cover with the School crest in the right hand corner. The *Kingstonian* 1989 was not only much larger, 68 full size A4 pages, with 27 photographs and 25 line drawings excitingly designed, but no less than eight pages, under the heading English/Art were given over to student Composition. Perhaps even more shocking for the traditionalists, the cover was of a young lady peering out at the world from behind a curtain. Like every subsequent cover this was the work of a member of the School. The Editor, Ian Stackhouse, said he expected a furious debate and made this comment as to the aim of the new-style magazine: *"Above all it has been an attempt to highlight the uniqueness of the very active life at KGS and also the special quality of its students and staff .... combining a serious approach in every sphere with a subtle streak of lightheartedness."* The old-style magazine was gone for ever.

The School Community

Three extra-mural organisations continued to attract the attention of large numbers of students. Indeed between them they continued to involve around half of the School population. All had been established since before the Second World War: the Gibbon Society, the CCF and the Christian Union.

Being a literary and cultural body the Gibbon Society was inclined to wax and wane according to the enthusiasms of the time. Thus in 1980 its Officers writing in the *Kingstonian* have to say *"During the past year the Gibbon Society has suffered one of the worst attacks of apathy in its history. The tireless efforts of*

Junior members of the School examine a Buccaneer in June 1984 at the RAF Air Display
Courtesy *Surrey Comet*

the Committee who undertook several new ventures were wasted by a total lack of support from the rest of the School." Even so there was a regular magazine, the *Nameless Mag*, regular debates, internal and inter-school, theatre visits and an Annual dinner. Just two years later the Society was once again thriving, the highlight of the year being their achievement in the Observer Mace School Debating Competition. The team reached the final round which was broadcast on Radio 4. A new House Debating Competition was launched, and the Junior Section of the Society revived. Whether or not it was *"the cultural Mecca of KGS"* as the writer of the 1987 report declared, the Gibbon Society was an invaluable part of the School's cultural life.

The Combined Cadet Force with its Army and Royal Air Force Sections continued to attract recruits, now of both sexes, and its weekly sessions, field days, Annual Inspection and Summer Camps went on uninterrupted. As the writer of the 1987 Report for the *Kingstonian* put it: *"The Combined Cadet Force machine ticks over still in it inimitable way. The field days both held on the Army exercise areas in Aldershot were as successful as one expects them to be and the Summer Camp held at Longmoor was a great event."*

The same year the RAF section report mentions that *"Everyone managed to fly during the course of the year at Abingdon,"* and that at a visit to RAF Northolt the party were escorted by Old Kingstonian Pilot Officer Janet Tuff. More flying, of course at summer camp rounded off the year.

The remarkable fact that for so many years the Christian Union, unlike its counterparts in some schools in Kingston, had not been a small slightly beleaguered group, away from the mainstream but a large and influential student body is perhaps due to two factors. First, it had always had encouragement from the top with the Headmaster's active support, and benefited from the guiding hand of successive masters whose Christian concerns helped to keep it on orthodox theological rails. Secondly, some School student leaders, prefects, sub prefects and sportsmen always played a part, giving the CU an "all right" image. Taking again the 1987 Report in the Magazine as typical, it tells of weekly Junior and Senior meetings with additional small study groups for each Year, a Senior houseparty at Christmas, and a Junior one at Easter with a summer Camp that *"attracted a record number of over a hundred and fifty, and the weather which was unusually good, permitted many activities ranging from mackerel fishing to three-legged football matches. The Lord blessed the evening meetings at which the claims of Christianity were presented."* Simply to list the more specialised clubs and societies is to confirm that nothing had changed since Her Majesty's Inspectors commented favourably on the great range of such activities back in 1958; Stamp Club, Radio Astronomy Society, Rifle Club, Wargames Society, The Social Union, Archaeological and Geological Society, Numismatic Society, Electronics Society, Photographic Society, Chess Society, Kingston Society, Bridge Club, Railway Enthusiasts' Society, Scientific Society, Dramatic Society, Subbuteo Society, Fell Walking Club, Historical and Geographical Society, Handicrafts Club, Natural History Club, Adventure Society, Social Services Group, and the Young Engineers' Club. And these were only the clubs that filed reports at some time in the 1970s and 1980s for the magazine!

One body re-established (though its earlier identity is misty) in 1977 was the Charities Committee, to co-ordinate efforts for outside giving. Its annual reports are a heartening record of the School's efforts to help others. Taking a single year as an exemplar; 1979-80 saw £700 raised by a stall at the Christmas Bazaar for the London Fund for the Blind and cards to the value of £300 were sold on behalf of various charities. $1^{1}/_{2}$ tonnes of newspaper were collected and sold for the National Kidney Research Fund; and a sponsored reading of *Paradise Lost* raised £400, later increased to £700, for the East African Famine Appeal.

Parents and Old Kingstonians

In the whole of the 20 year period between 1970 and 1991 no report from the Parent Staff Association appears in the *Kingstonian*. Either they never thought to contribute or they were never invited to do so. Only passing references to fetes and bazaars and to the part played by individuals in the Music Society and in the KGS Choral Society indicated the existence of around 1000 parents in the background. The PSA did of course have representation on the Governing Body and produced its own annual reports, but the lack of partici-pation in the School's own official record is surprising.

By contrast, the Old Kingstonians contributed to the *Kingstonian* without fail. If its litany of Open Days, AGMs, annual dinners, and the activities of golfers and hockey players was inevitably somewhat repetitious, the OK Directory with its details of Old Kingstonians' individual activities was not. But in the rampant inflation of the mid seventies the Association needed funds to keep going. First they put the subscription up from £1 to £2.50. Some members paid up, a few resigned and a lot more just left their banker's orders at £1, convinced, correctly of course, that the Treasurer would not delete their names from the list! There had to be a better way of funding the Association. There was. The Governors approved a scheme, under which a small sum was added each term to the pupils' fees and paid into a capital fund held by the Bursar. Then, when a student left the School a lump sum was handed over to the Association, to fund that individual's lifetime membership. So, from 1980 everyone leaving KGS after a full School career has been a life member receiving the Association's literature and, if they wish, the *Kingstonian*. At a stroke the problem of membership and funding was solved, though it has to be said the number of active members remains small, even though nominal membership now approaches 2000.

Conclusion

The 1970s and 1980s were a period of major change, from direct grant status to independence and from single sex to co-educational status. It was well managed. And it was achieved without any slow-down in progress academically or in the field of sports. If that progress was sometimes less dramatic than in earlier years, it reflected the fact that the scope for further improvement in some spheres was becoming limited. The nearer one gets to 100% success in exam results the less room remains for improvement. If the Hockey teams and oarsmen and women are winning many trophies already, their best efforts and best coaching may not be able to take them a great deal further.

However, KGS has never been a school whose reputation has rested solely on such factors. Way back in the 19th century when William Rigg was Headmaster, and the School operated in the cramped quarters of the Chapel it had a reputation as a happy place. At that time it was incompetent, but happy, according to the Inspectors! Academic competence gradually replaced incompetence, but the fact that KGS was a happy School remained, to be commented on by Inspectors over the next century. And there is no doubt that the three successive Heads in the 70s and 80s, Messrs Strover, Miller and Creber continued in this spirit. Indeed it might be said that a school community with so much music in the air was bound to be a happy one. The comment in the *Kingstonian* of 1989 also rings true; the special quality of students and staff at KGS is the ability to combine a serious approach in every sphere with *"a subtle streak of lightheartedness"*.

CHAPTER 12

—··◆··—

On to the Millennium
(1991-1999)

—··◆··—

IN SEPTEMBER 1991 DUNCAN BAXTER arrived to be the new Headmaster at KGS. Aged 37, and an Oxford MA, he came to the school from Wycliffe College in Gloucestershire, where he had been Academic Director and Head of Sixth Form. His teaching subject was English and he was a Fellow the Royal Society of Arts. Interviewed for the *Kingstonian* shortly after his arrival he said that his main reason for joining the school was *"because it is one of the best schools in the country. It has a national reputation for academic and sporting excellence and I wanted to go to a top school"*. In answer to the question "What particular aspects of the school would you like to change and improve?" he made it clear however that the school could not rest on its laurels.

"I still think there is a long way to go on the academic excellence. Even though we had good results last year, these results are, rightly or wrongly a way in which the school is judged, so we have got to get this right. To do this we must improve the facilities, the teaching methods and perhaps even the format of the timetable."

Academic Excellence

By 1998, boys and girls who were at the bottom of the school when the new Head took over in 1991 were now taking their A Level exams and the Headmaster was able to tell those at the Annual Prize Giving that the A Level pass rate was 99%, with 63% of entries at A or B grades. No less than 13 pupils had gained three or more A grades (six boys and seven girls). At GCSE level all 92 students gained five or more A-C grades, 30 of them getting at least seven or more A* or A grades. With some justifiable pride the Head wrote in the *Kingstonian* that in both *The Times* and the *Telegraph's* analyses KGS was in the top quarter of all HMC schools for A level results.

A year later results were even better with 100% success at A level, 66% at A

Duncan Baxter,
Headmaster from 1991

or B grade; and the GCSE results were equally outstanding with all 97 candidates obtaining at least 5 A-C passes, 40 of them getting 7 or more A grades: 56% of all entries were A⋆ or A.

In 1998 Duncan Baxter was elected to the National Committee of the Headmasters' and Headmistresses' Conference from the beginning of 1999 and to the Chairmanship of its London Division in the year 2000. What a transformation from the school which His Majesty's Inspectors saw back in 1914 when they commented in their Inspection Report that they found the school *"not inefficient but wholly lacking in distinction".* They held out no great hopes for the future of KGS. *"If the school is to do first grade work, it is essential its financial position should be still further improved ....and the defects of its buildings improved."*

The Inspectors expressed the hope that such improvements would occur! Such damning remarks were not surprising, when the Inspectors found that of 130 boys who left the school between 1905 and 1913, an eight year period, *"none went from the school direct to one of the older Universities"* a performance or rather non-performance light years away from what developed from the 1920s onwards as the School grew in numbers and academic prowess. In 1999 alone, ten students went on to Oxford and Cambridge.

The 1995 Inspection of the School

None of Duncan Baxter's predecessors since Percy Rundle had had to cope with a full scale Inspection. The last one was in 1957. Another might have been due at the end of the 1970s, but by then KGS was independent, and as such subject neither to the old-style Inspections by HMIs nor to the subsequent OFSTED regime. However, the Headmasters' and Headmistresses' Conference runs its own School Inspection Service and the Headmaster invited them, with the agreement of the Governors, to come and conduct a full inspection. A team which was ten strong spent a whole week at the school in March 1995. Led by the Headmaster of Stockport Grammar School, the team of generalists and subject specialists

"observed 163 lessons, visited Ditton Field and the river, attended assemblies and tutor periods, rehearsals, societies and an impressive range of extra curricular activities. The inspection team attended 58 planned meetings with the Senior Management Group, Head of every Department, the Bursar and key non-teaching staff. A meeting with parents organised by the PSA enabled the inspectors to ascertain the view of parents informally. The written work of three pupils in each year group was examined and discussed with the pupils." (Summary Report)

And the conclusions drawn from this intensive review? There were of course recommendations for improvement, for instance in what the Inspectors called *"spiritual and cultural appreciation and understanding"*. The School needed to establish a clear marking policy to be enforced by every Department. Management and leadership functions of heads of Departments should be emphasised and reinforced.

But overall the Report warmly commended the School, summarised in the first main finding, *"Kingston Grammar School is a happy, friendly, open school with a hardworking staff, purposeful pupils and appreciative parents."* They went on to say that the School achieved highly creditable results, and was sensitive to the needs of individual pupils. In classrooms the atmosphere was purposeful and the pupils co-operative, well motivated and keen to succeed. The School should take pride, the Inspectors concluded, in the standard achieved by its pupils and their quality of learning. It is on the Report's findings (it runs to 186 paragraphs) that the School's further development is being successfully based, as the latest academic results show.

The Inspectors had good things to say about the School community as well. There was, they said, a rich range of extra mural activities strongly supported by teachers. Moreover, *"the pupils are considerate to each other, and have positive attitudes to the school. There is no evidence of any bullying. They are open, friendly, and accommodating; they can readily identify adults to whom they would turn if in need of help or advice."*

Building in the 1990s

One of the Inspectors' Recommendations raised a wry smile amongst Governors and Staff alike. It was this, *"Any further building and refurbishment should be based on a coherent integrated development plan for the whole school site"*.

The 1988 Development Programme Appeal resulted in new buildings, including a
(*top*) Library, (*above*) Art Gallery and (*facing page*) Lecture Theatre

On a constricted town centre site there has always been a severe limitation on what building can be done. Indeed this very fact was a major reason for some Governors' enthusiasm to move the school out of Kingston altogether and on to Ditton Field, in the 1960s and early 70s. The Chairman of the Governors went on record in 1965 as saying there was very little scope for new building at London Road. In fact, a remarkable record of building works was undertaken in the next 25 years and this continued in the 1990s. A suite of classrooms was built on the roof of the gymnasium and a substantial IT centre constructed within the existing Fairfield buildings. A modern languages suite rounded off these developments in September 1999. New kitchens, a reordered Dining Room, and for the first time a proper Reception Area came into being at the London Road end, in the old 19th century range. What is clear is that whilst a master plan is always useful, how it is implemented depends on opportunity and ingenuity, the latter being very much to the fore in the thinking, over the whole period since the 60s, of the school's design duo, John Snelling, Old Kingstonian (1947-51) and building consultant, and Lewis Barker, Architect. The School owes them much. What is certain, however, is that it will never be possible to expand the facilities to meet the needs of more than the existing 600 pupils; but that may be no bad thing.

The School Community

The Inspectors commented very favourably on the range of extra curricular activities, visiting 19 activities over just three days. They particularly liked the

The opening of the new ICT Centre in 1998 by the Mayor of Kingston upon Thames

fact that pupils felt sufficiently confident to take the initiative and organise sessions for themselves. Indeed this aspect of school life continued to flourish through the decade. At the heart were the Combined Cadet force, the Christian Union, whose summer camps remained as popular as ever, attracting no less than 150 to Brixham in 1998, and the Gibbon Society who held their Centenary dinner at the end of 1997. Art and Music flourished; the School raised £4500 that year for charities. The Duke of Edinburgh's Award Scheme had 25 sixth formers involved at Gold level. Annual productions of the Choral Society through the 90s, parents, pupils and teachers, included Haydn's Creation, and Bach's Mass in B Minor. The Dramatic Society Senior plays continued to show a range exceptional for school productions, from David Hare's *Racing Demons* and Harold Pinter's *The Hothouse* to *Othello* and *Guys and Dolls*.

Throughout the period, too, the Parent Staff Association and the Old Kingstonian Association continued to give substantial support to the School, as well as to provide opportunities for social activity. For instance the PSA gave the School £7745 in the year 1994-95 covering the cost amongst other things of a Camcorder, Mac notebook, lights for the drama department, climbing gear and safety equipment. The OKA in the second half of the decade were also able to contribute from their funds nearly £20,000, including a donation of £10,000 to the 1998 Development Appeal, the first fruits of which were used to construct an Information Technology Centre and whole school network. As the Head indicated this was all part of *"positioning the School to be one of the best equipped and most successful independent schools in the country in the new millennium."* In the sporting field the School's record in the 90s equalled or bettered any past period (see Chapter 15).

Nor should the continuing role of the Lovekyn Chantry Lodge, which celebrated its fiftieth anniversary in 1999 be overlooked. Over a hundred members and guests from other Lodges attended a special meeting and a souvenir brochure of the history of the Lodge was produced. The School has recently granted the Lodge a lease to use the refurbished Chapel for its meetings, for a period of 14 years. This gives them security for the future. Former pupils, parents and staff are all eligible to join the Lodge.

A First Choice School

Among the Headmaster's aims for the school was "to make KGS first choice for pupils and parents". This meant a thorough overhaul of every aspect of school life.

School Development Plans enabled forward thinking to cope with the expectations of pupils and parents in the 1990s. Among the initiatives which came from this thinking was the appointment of a Development Director to raise funds on a continuous basis rather than have stop-go appeals. The "Appeal in Pursuit of New Excellence" begun in 1998 saw the start of this process. The abolition of Assisted Places in 1997 caused fears that the number of pupils in the school would be reduced and the school would lose its breadth of social and cultural backgrounds which had been its hallmark during direct grant days. Fortunately, the number of pupils registering for admission at 11+ increased rather than decreased and the Governors agreed to put aside money for means tested bursaries so that lack of money did not have to be a bar to entry for able children who would benefit from being at the school. Numbers increased in the 1990s from 580 to 605+ with academic, art, music, sport and 6th form scholarships available.

On the curricular front, Spanish was added as a modern language and a multi-media languages laboratory was added in 1999. Technology, drama, politics and sports studies were among subjects added or developed anew at the school. Time was set aside also for tutorial work and for a personal and social education programme.

As far as the staff were concerned, a system of appraisal and professional review was put in place together with annual target setting for departments and regular internal reviews of all departments. The Investors in People Award achieved in 1999 helped to give a framework to much of this development. A Working Party also looked at the working of the Governing Body and many ideas designed to improve communication between the staff and Governors, and parents and Governors were put in place, together with a change to the Constitution of the school allowing it to do more than teach

(*Left*) Mr P R Ekberg, Old Kingstonian and former Chairman of Governors, September 1988–September 1996

(*Centre*) Dr A J H Mercer, Chairman of Governors since 1996

(*Bottom*) Commemoration Day Service 1997 Canon Roger Royle, Mr C D Baxter Headmaster, Deputy Mayor and wife, Dr A J H Mercer, Chairman of Governors and the Vicar of St. Peters Norbiton

only boys and girls! The idea was to earn money from courses held, for example, in the new Information and Communication Technology Centre and the letting of school facilities — all part of the need to increase school funds. The Senior Management Group of staff was restructured to form an Executive, to work more closely with Governors on sub-committees.

Better communication was, in fact, the key to much of what changed. A senior member of staff was appointed Director of External Relations, which led to regular promotional material being sent to the Press, to the institution of a three-times-a-year publication sent to all Old Kingstonians and the installation of a Website on the Internet. Much work was done to forge links with feeder schools, including many local primary schools, work which was reinforced by the Government's support for partnership between independent and maintained schools. Current pupils at the school were not forgotten and a School Forum enabled representatives from all the tutor groups to meet the Headmaster twice a term to make suggestions about the school, and bring to his attention any ideas they might have for improvement.

Commemorating the School's Benefactors

Every year the School holds a service in church to commemorate its benefactors. Either a former pupil or a distinguished outsider speaks of what is owed to those whose generosity helped secure the School's future. First and foremost amongst benefactors stands Queen Elizabeth I whose charters of 1561 and 1564 founded, and endowed the School. The rents from these lands and properties were to meet the salaries of the Master and Usher for the next 3 centuries.

But what Queen Elizabeth I gave for the foundation of her Grammer School at Kingston was, almost entirely, what had been confiscated in 1547 when Lovekyn Chapel and all its endowments were forfeit to the Crown. Richard Taverner then leases them from the Crown; in 1564 he gave up his lease in favour of the new School. And of course, those same lands and properties had been donated in the 14th Century by Edward and John Lovekyn and by Sir William Walworth to provide for the chaplains at the Lovekyn Chantry Chapel. So the School looks right back each year to these 14th century donors; and it recalls not only major benefactors, but also the many more who have contributed over the years towards the School's growth and well-being.

A New Role for the Chapel

Until 1992 the Lovekyn Chapel was in use as a Woodwork shop, a function which an earlier Headmaster, Sidney Miller, had said at Speech Day was particularly appropriate since Jesus had been a carpenter. But the arrival of Technology as a curriculum subject tolled the deathknoll for traditional craft activities like woodwork. With the construction of a Technology Centre next to

Chapel as Woodwork Shop before restoration

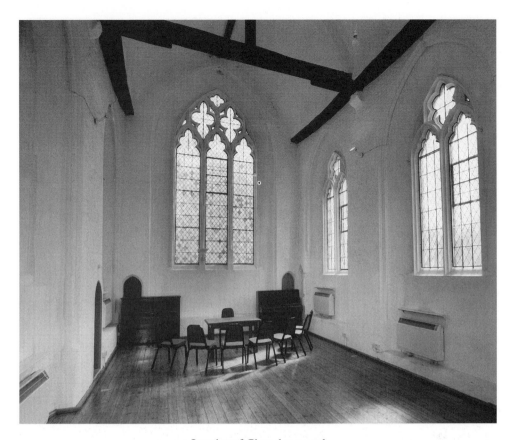

Interior of Chapel restored

the new Art Department the Chapel fell empty. Since 1561 it had been used for teaching purposes and even after the new school buildings were opened in 1878 continued to be a valuable resource, at various times the sixth form room, the School gymnasium, home of the Prep form and of the Junior library.

Now there was the opportunity to restore this unique 14th Century chapel to something like its pristine state, to be used for music and the arts, not just by the School but by the people of Kingston as well. A committee of trustees, "town and gown", was set up to launch the Lovekyn Chapel Appeal with a target of £150,000 to restore the Chapel and its adjacent two storey cottage, which was to provide refurbished music practice rooms, cloakrooms and a small kitchen, whilst the surroundings would be paved and landscaped.

Grants from English Heritage, from the National Lottery, from several major Trusts, and from many individuals enabled the trustees to go ahead with the work (the Chapel is of course a starred Grade 2 listed building) the final touches, the landscaping, being completed in the summer of 1999. The building remains part of the School's freehold but now will serve the needs of the wider community as well.

(*Left*) Ceremonial entrance of The Swan at the Lovekyn Feast, September 1999

(*Bottom left*) Four Guests at the Lovekyn Feast: Mr David Smedley (First Chairman of the Lovekyn Trustees), his wife Lesley and extreme right, Mr John McCarthy (Current Chairman of trustees) and his wife Pat

(*Right*) The Lovekyn Feast menu

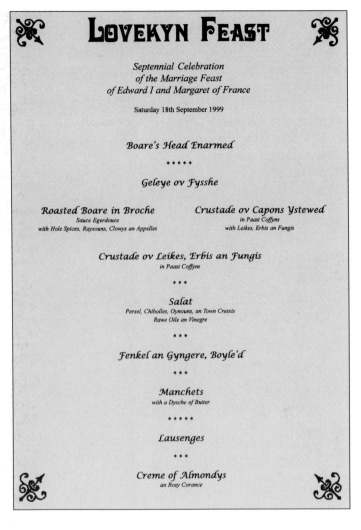

LOVEKYN FEAST

*Septennial Celebration
of the Marriage Feast
of Edward I and Margaret of France*

Saturday 18th September 1999

Boare's Head Enarmed

✦ ✦ ✦ ✦ ✦

Geleye ov Fysshe

Roasted Boare in Broche
Sauce Egerdouce
with Hole Spices, Raysouns, Clowys an Appelles

Crustade ov Capons Ystewed
in Paast Coffyns
with Leikes, Erbis an Fungis

Crustade ov Leikes, Erbis an Fungis
in Paast Coffyns

✦ ✦ ✦

Salat
Persel, Chibolles, Oynouns, an Town Cressis
Rawe Oile an Vinegre

✦ ✦ ✦

Fenkel an Gyngere, Boyle'd

✦ ✦ ✦

Manchets
with a Dysche of Butter

✦ ✦ ✦ ✦ ✦

Lausenges

✦ ✦ ✦

Creme of Almondys
an Rosy Corance

It had been just 700 years before this restoration of the Chapel that Edward and Robert Lovekyn, caterers of Kingston, had provided the wedding banquet for Edward I's marriage to Margaret of France, on 16th September 1299. Had the King paid up there would have been no chantry chapel, for it was only as a rare royal favour in return for remitting the debt that Edward Lovekyn was permitted to build his personal chapel ten years later. And when the citizens of Kingston appealed to Queen Elizabeth I for a school it was, to say the least, fortuitous that the Chapel which like all other religious houses had become forfeit to the Crown was empty and available to be the Schoolroom. What is more the Chapel's endowments went in large part to fund the new Grammar School.

149

The link between what happened in 1299 and the 600 strong school which stands on the very site of the Chapel meadow is a unique one. For certain no other school in the country has a medieval Chantry Chapel as part of its inheritance or can look back to such unusual beginnings. So it was appropriate that there should be a great festivity, the Lovekyn Feast, in full medieval splendour held in the Chapel and then the Hall, to commemorate, 700 years later on 18th September 1999, the wedding feast on which the School's fortunes depended so much. The next great Commemoration will be the founding of the Chapel itself, the 700th anniversary of which is in 2009!

SPORTS AT KINGSTON GRAMMAR SCHOOL

GORDON EVANS

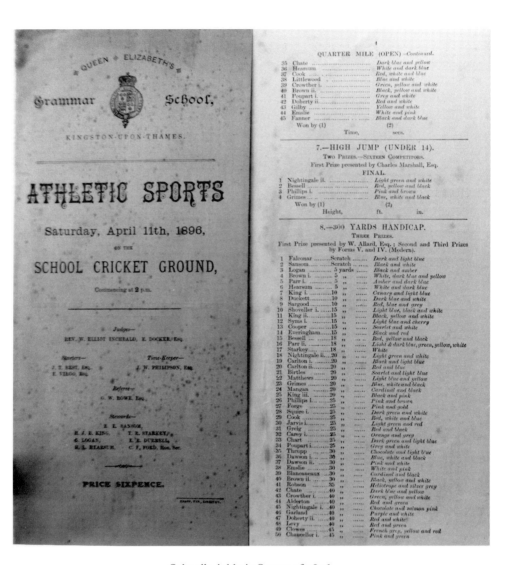

School's Athletic Sports of 1896

CHAPTER 13

—··◆··—

Sport before the 1914-1918 War

—··◆··—

I N THE AUTUMN OF 1920 two sixth formers paid a visit to an Old Boy, the Rev J W Maunders and asked him to talk about KGS as it had been fifty years before. He began by remarking that by the standards of the 1920s the school had been something of a farce. There had been some seventy or eighty boys herded into the Chapel and subjected to a severe course of Latin and the stick by the Staff, namely the Headmaster and an assistant. When asked about Games he expostulated thus: *"Games! No, we had no organised games at all. I think all the boys were so glad to get away from the school that they did not come back until the last possible moment. I believe that sometimes a few boys turned up with hockey sticks on Saturday and knocked a ball about on the Field but that was all that was ever done."* Apparently such unorganised hockey came about since there was insufficient space behind the School for a proper football pitch. We know from brief reminiscences that in his heyday, in the 1860s, the then Headmaster the Reverend William Rigg had shown an interest in sport even to the point of joining in but in the later days of his Headship numbers shrank until when he handed over to Reverend W E Inchbald in 1883, there were only twenty three boys. They could at best have engaged as boys over the Ages have done in some desultory game of football, or as in this particular case, hockey. Indeed it may have been in order to introduce an element of variety or simply to provide a relaxation more suitable for limited numbers that William Rigg turned the dormitory into a billiards room. Things in short could only get better.

The Influence of Inchbald

Three elements are essential if games are to flourish in any school, namely substantial numbers of pupils, suitable facilities and the presence of able, keen and willing Staff. Inchbald succeeded in acquiring all three, though he was rather more successful in obtaining suitable staff than in providing good pitches. It is a bonus if the Headmaster, like Charles Aubrey Howse of later years, is also keen and knowledgeable himself. Howse was to be found, umbrella in hand, behind the nets at the School's Dinton Road Sports Field demonstrating the appropriate cricket shots. Inchbald for his part was involved in judging the Rowing inter alia. He was fortunate to have in Mr Docker, his Second Master, and Mr Best, an Assistant Master, two of a long succession of Masters (extending unbroken to the present day) who have given their services without stinting in the interests of School Games. Indeed the appointment of such men (and women) is never far from every Headmaster's mind. There were of course no Houses in the pre-war period and internal competition was between the Classical and Modern sides. In order to regulate, and pay for, such contests and matches involving other schools, Inchbald instituted a Games Committee and a Games fund, the latter drawing on subscriptions and the proceeds of entry charges to the Athletic Sports, topped up from time to time with money raised by concerts and social events.

The Games Committee

The Games Committee was presided over by the Headmaster and consisted of Masters and a handful of senior boys. In 1910 there were six Masters, two boys and the members of the Upper Sixth. As the number and scope of games increased so did the size of the Committee; by the 1970s it was very large indeed and a good deal of horse-trading took place when anything controversial arose. As is the way in situations of this kind the wishes of an inner Cabal tended to prevail. Nevertheless the democratic element was of value even when many suspected a stronger force for benevolent dictatorship. What could be frustrating for those charged with responsibility, who in many cases had been in that position for many years, was the tendency for the same debate to recur with what seemed like monotonous regularity, with each fresh generation of boys arguing the case for such things as a review of House Points with new vigour. Nothing it seems was too small to escape the Committee's attention. Minutes from 1911 record for example that *"the points for the Form Shield be divided by the number of boys not absolutely incapable of running on the day of the Sports"*; those of 11th May 1916 lay down inter alia that *"in the Slow Bicycle Race no competitor may lock his wheel but must always advance towards the tape"*, that in Throwing the Cricket Ball *"no run longer than six yards be allowed"* and that *"prizes for Senior and Junior races be medals only, while those for Handicaps and other races be such things as pencil cases and penknives."* The election of the officials of various Clubs, the awarding of School Colours, the naming of those deemed to be regular members of the 1st Elevens, the appointment of selection committees to pick the two top Elevens, who incidentally were told on one occasion *"to inspect the Field the night before the match to see if rolling be necessary"* other preliminaries having already been done by the Prefects aided by boys from the Remove, all these fell within the Committee's jurisdiction. In addition it laid down hours of play, and the

Ist XI Cricket team c. 1900 – 7 boys and 4 masters including Deputy Head

number of fixtures. A limit of ten was placed on those for 1st XI cricket in 1916 all of which were against local schools including Tiffin's, St George's Weybridge, Hampton Grammar School, Rutlish, Sutton County and Richmond County, names which recur over a very long period. When Carter I had played in an Intermediate House match between Queen's and Walworth while a member of the First Eleven, the Committee ordered the match to be replayed. In the years before 1914 a number of ticklish issues presented themselves, including one in 1911 when Mr Etches proposed that Tiffins be written to, asking if an ex-pupil Cook could be allowed to row at the regatta as he had left School. This motion was carried but unfortunately we do not know what the response was. When Mr Etches proposed in February 1914 the creation of three Houses; Lovekyn, Queen's and Walworth, with the consequential House Championship (later extended by the creation of a fourth House, Taverner), producing a gradual increase in the number of games played, he opened up new fields of almost endless debate, sometime quite acrimonious. How did one decide whether Junior hockey matches were worth more or fewer House points than House Fours or Junior Cross Country? How indeed! Was Squash worthy of inclusion in the Competition and if so could those concerned demonstrate their ability to run such a competition satisfactorily? These were questions which would run and run. Many a heated discussion in the old Library was brought to a conclusion only by the ringing of the bell at 1.55 pm.

From exceedingly small beginnings the joint influences of the Reverend Inchbald and Mr Docker created a framework of sporting activities. In the first year, 1883, cricket took pride of place, appropriately it would seem since Mr Docker was to become a stalwart of the School First Eleven for nearly twenty years as batsman, wicketkeeper and sometime bowler. Sixteen matches were played including two against Hampton Wick Royal CC. Other than these only a few anonymous games of Rugby Football took place. Within four years, swimming in the river, a limited amount of Drill, and Athletic Sports held on Surbiton Recreation Ground for the first time in 1887, took up the chase. Among the events forming part of the Sports was a one mile walking handicap race. Difficulty was experienced in finding Rugby Football fixtures and once Soccer was introduced in 1887 Rugby was soon abandoned altogether. Boxing classes were organised in 1889-1890. Two Fours, one representing the Classical and the other the Modern Side, formed part of the

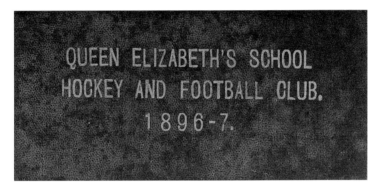

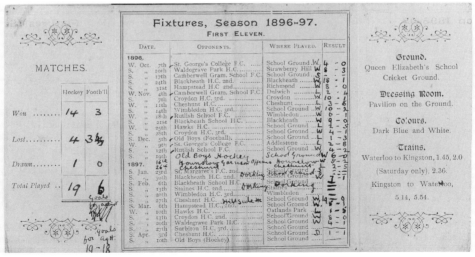

The Hockey and Football Club fixture list for Season 1896–7

Kingston Borough Regatta, a link that was maintained for many years, and a Cross Country was run after a number of paperchases had proved popular in the Autumn Term. Things continued to move on apace: the 1891 Sports were held on a newly-acquired playing field in Oil Mill Lane, where a pavilion had just been erected and paid for by subscription, and hockey made its appearance. In 1892, the School held its first Regatta which included sculling, an Old Boys' punt race and single and double Canadian Canoe races. Numbers were by now well over a hundred and in the Sports of 1893 no fewer than forty boys ran in the 300 yards Handicap.

Small wonder that in his Speech Day Address in 1894 the Headmaster was moved to speak eloquently of the School's progress and prowess on the Games field. *"With regard to games,"* he said, *"in football we had quite the best team which the School has ever produced and in hockey we did not lose a single match. Our Athletic Sports in April were attended by a very large company .... a great success .... out of ten cricket matches played so far by the First Eleven we have won seven."* By the end of the cricket season the side had won ten matches and the Second Eleven had won six. Opponents included the oldest of 'old enemies' St George's Weybridge, Camberwell Grammar School, Arlington College, Chiswick, Hampton Wick Royal CC 2nd XI and East Molesey 2nd XI. The footballers in winning seven matches out of twelve met St George's, Camberwell, East Molesey and Guildford Grammar School. Only six First Eleven hockey matches were played, all in the Spring Term. Of these five were won and opponents included Teddington, West Ealing and Surbiton Hockey Clubs. On the river, two Regattas took place in that academic year, one in September and the other in the following July. The Old Boys had asked for the timing to be changed as they said that the summer would be more convenient for them. The Register commented, *"it cannot be said, however that the result was satisfactory seeing that few Old Boys evinced any interest in the fixture either by entering the races, i.e. Past v Present or in any other way."* Many years later Old Kingstonians persuaded the Master in charge of cricket to forsake the by then customary date for the Past v Present fixture which was Whit Monday and adopt a Saturday near the end of the Summer Term. The result was much the same as it had been all those years before with little or no increase in the number of spectators and little decrease in the difficulty in raising the Old Boys' side! The Regattas consisted of the mixture as before, plus a Dongola Race. In the Borough Regatta, the School was allocated a sculling race in which seven boys took part, a four-oared Race between Classical and Modern and another four-oared race against Hampton Grammar School, but they for reasons unknown declined the offer. The boats were supplied by Turks and the Headmaster acted as umpire, assisted by other members of Staff. The Headmaster was also in evidence, this time as judge when the three swimming races were held between the two bridges on the Hampton Wick bank of the Thames at 7 am on 27th July 1894.

The day of the Athletic Sports, the timing of which vacillated over the years between the Spring Term which was often cold and wet and the Summer Term where it interfered with cricket, was 21st April in 1894 and clearly one of the highlights of the School year. The programme contained the bones of a modern Sports Day; there were twenty races including various sprints, a quarter mile, a mile, long and high jumps, a Jockey Race, throwing the cricket ball and a tug-of-war. In addition to the cup for Victor Ludorum, a Perseverance Prize went to the competitor taking part in the largest number of events without winning a prize. After a long lapse such a trophy was reinstated in the 1960s under the title of the Sportsman's Cup. Plus ça change. The last sporting event in the Reverend Inchbald's survey, Cross Country, was run over a course of seven miles taking in Chessington, Worcester Park and Berrylands. Old Boys acted as markers and areas of ploughed field are mentioned. In the following year the course measured eleven miles and the winning time was one hour, one minute and fifteen seconds. The juniors ran a shorter course in Bushey Park. There was in addition a Drill Competition, defined as physical exercises with and without arms, horizontal and parallel bars, ropes, dumbbells and singlestick. Prizes awarded included two pairs of foils. When much later House Drill and Shooting became part of the House Championship it was a Cadet Force prerogative.

The End of Football

Perhaps the most significant change to take place in the years before 1914 was the decision to abandon football and play only hockey throughout the winter Terms. Given the general popularity of soccer and the cachet held by some to attach itself to rugby this is a little surprising for a School on the up and up. Even more surprising was the rapidity of the change; in a matter of three years football went from equal status into oblivion. From a point when there were more football fixture than hockey fixtures, the position was reversed within two years and hockey had crept into the Autumn Term, though admittedly for only a single match. The following season, 1896-1897 hockey was played equally alongside football and proved the more popular; in the season 1897-1898 the Register records that there were only two football matches, both of them against St George's College Weybridge. The first game was most remarkable as not only did we take to Addlestone a team which had not played for a year, but we were one short at half back. Despite these disadvantages we won a fine match by four goals to one. The battle had been won but the war lost.

Hockey Triumphant

Hockey had triumphed and in its first solo season the First Eleven won eleven out of twenty four matches played while the Second Eleven won four out of seven. It continued to flourish even when School numbers fell below a hundred after the turn of the century and in 1911 there were no fewer than forty two matches on the card. The Second Eleven in 1911 played some fifteen matches and from time to time a small number of junior matches were arranged, sometimes against local girls schools. Compared to the relatively consistent fixture lists of say, the 1960s and 1970s there is an enormous variety to be found in these early days. The majority of matches were against Clubs, which was inevitable since other schools did not play the game in the Autumn Term but some names familiar in more recent times are to be found, though St George's Weybridge is the only one to maintain an unbroken record down to the end of the twentieth century. Of other familiar names most are still extant and include Battersea Polytechnic, Spencer, Hawks, Blackheath, Southgate, Surbiton, Hampstead, Staines and Teddington. The norm was for the School 1st XI to play one of their lower elevens, usually the second eleven. Matches against the Old Boys were a regular feature and sometimes twice in the same season. As with the cricket sides, Masters played to stiffen the boys though there seem to have been fewer in the hockey than in the cricket teams. This practice continued down to the outbreak of the war. In 1907 the School acquired a valuable fullback in Mr F St A Rogers who had won a Half Blue at Cambridge while in 1908 Mr Keech the choirmaster played. In 1907 it was decided to reward regular First Eleven players with a hockey cap *"half red and half grey with crossed sticks and a ball in front"*.

Old Boy Successes

Gradually the School's reputation for hockey spread as Old Boys made their mark in Club sides, then in County and Divisional sides and finally in the rarefied regions of Internationals and Olympics. Parr played for Middlesex in 1898 and S H Shoveller in 1899. The latter went on to play for England in 1902, won two Olympic Gold Medals and finally retired in 1921 with thirty six caps having scored on each occasion he played and scoring in all nearly a hundred goals. In 1909 E A C Thomson writing in the *Illustrated Sporting and Dramatic News* described Shoveller as *"the greatest exponent of hockey forward play the game has so far produced."* In 1904 four Old Kingstonians played for London against the United Universities, Shoveller, G Logan, C S Burge and N T Nightingale and in 1908 Logan was in the Olympic Squad.

Playground Hockey

This is perhaps the point at which to pause and consider the cause of both the strength and weaknesses of School hockey. The explanation lies in the tradition of pickup games in the playground. It is significant that the Reverend Maunders in his scathing reference to games in 1870 does not say, as one might imagine knowing the ordinary boy's propensity for kicking everything in sight to the detriment of his footwear as every parent knows, that the boys came in on a Saturday to play football amongst themselves. Instead he says

The Annual Cross Country Race, 1906

that they played with hockey sticks. This undoubtedly continued until we find in 1920 in 'Hockey', under the heading Famous Hockey Schools, Kingston Grammar School referred to thus: *"the chief feature of the School game is polished stickwork and this is probably attributable to the 'pick-up' game played in all spare minutes on the gravel."*

Much earlier, in 1905 we find references to the fitting of felt and wire-netting to the wooden railings in the playground where it adjoined private houses in order to deaden the sound of the hockey balls and *"so lessen the inconvenience of our neighbours,"* while in 1909 the announcement came that the playground was to be covered in gravel, a pre-echo one feels of the ongoing difference of opinion between the School and the residents near Ditton Field which in turn led to an attempt to deaden the sound of the ball striking the backboards in one of the goals. In short, stickwork was almost entirely self-taught and those who coached could concentrate on positional play and tactics once the small boy had been initiated into the rudiments of this new mystery.

A feature of the School Magazine of the time, the *Register*, was detailed reports of certain matches, sometimes the contest between Classical and Modern, sometimes matches against the Old Boys. In addition cameo sketches of 11 team members, 'characters' as they came to be known, both for hockey and for cricket made their appearance and continued to appear down to the 1970s when the need to limit magazine space led to their disappearance.

Not for their authors, the masters in charge, those platitudinous fall-backs of ordinary school reports, 'could do better', 'fair', 'satisfactory' or 'very fair'. The characters probed more deeply, though one does occasionally come across a gem like *"he should endeavour to bat better"* or this from 1895 *"Caulton II tried early in the season as a long-stop and proving himself fearless in this position speedily became a fixture"*, a comment which probably tells us more about the accuracy of the bowling and the state of the outfield than it does about the unfortunate Caulton II, condemned by his desperate devotion to duty rather like the Flying Dutchman to plod his way over after over from one end of the field to the other. One of the most common comments was that, far from not having mastered the tricky art of close control of a small white ball with a bent stick on a muddy, bumpy surface, all too many Kingstonians had mastered it all too well for the common good. In truth if there is one weakness in Kingston's hockey common to both nineteenth and twentieth centuries, it is over-elaborate stickwork leading to the wish, as one spectator put it *"to walk the ball into the net"*.

Cricket

Cricket was not so easy. Much intensive coaching and practice was necessary and sound surfaces were essential. We are all too familiar with the sight of the tentative schoolboy edging away towards the square leg umpire as the fast bowler walks back to the end of his run. It is clear that good wickets were at a premium in Inchbald's day and beyond. There are references to various grounds in use before the acquisition of Dinton Road in 1926: matches were played on 'the school field in Oil Mill Lane' in the 1880s, but by 1906 the Magazine bewails the absence 'of a ground of our own' and other facilities had to be obtained in Richmond Park, Home Park, Bushey Park and the Fairfield which was at the time also Tiffin's home ground. Lack of suitable pitches reduced the fixture list to a mere seven matches in 1907 though the Magazine hopefully recorded *'that next season we may have a proper groundsman'*. It must be said that when in occupation of Oil Mill Lane there was always one groundsman and sometimes two. To prove the point the Old Boys' match in 1907 was won but the scores make depressing reading: the School made fifty of which Mr Cocks made twenty and the Old Boys were dismissed for fourteen. It was said that Mr Collier proposed to hold 'nets' in the playground the following season. The batting had clearly suffered from the departure of Mr Docker in 1902 after twenty one years service. His influence no doubt lived on but his place at the crease was not easily filled. The coincidence of Mr Docker and the ground at Oil Mill Lane had produced a significant flowering of the summer game, the high point of which was probably 1896 when the School won thirteen of its nineteen games and in doing so exceeded a hundred runs no fewer than eight times. The most impressive performance, always bearing in mind Disraeli's apposite dictum on statistics, was the annihilation of Emanuel School. The School had batted first and reached two hundred and seventeen; they then bowled out the opposition for nineteen. Hearsum ended the season having scored four hundred and thirty eight runs at an average of 26.76 and King II had taken eighty seven wickets at a cost of just under five apiece.

Declining Standards 1890–1914

A downturn so far as cricket is concerned may perhaps be detected in the season preceding Mr Docker's departure when the eleven only reached a hundred five times. By this time numbers were declining and the loss of even one key player could have grave consequences. The season 1909 saw the School score a mere fourteen against Manor House School and the ultimate degradation must have been when the side was dismissed for six by a Tiffin eleven who had already made two hundred and thirty two for the lost of only two wickets. In all fairness it has to be said that Kingston beat Tiffin's in a return match by eighty six runs to sixty. There is no record of any cricket at all in 1910.

Other Games in the Period through to 1914

The state of other games in the immediate pre-war era was at best cyclical, though hockey seems to have suffered less than the rest. The annual School Athletics survived more or less intact throughout with about twenty events each year. In addition to those now considered fit for inclusion in a serious meeting were events in keeping with the festive nature of Sports Day. A selection of the following was to be found: a Lilliputian Race, a Donkey Race, a Sack Race, a two-mile bicycle Race, a Tug-of-War (sometimes Classical v Modern, sometimes Middlesex v Surrey or School v Old Boys) and a Victorian Cross Race. This last caused *"much merriment as the negotiation of some railings by the boys who were laden with full-size dummies of straw gave rise to many spills and their return journey on bicycles .... was by no means the shortest distance between two points."* On one occasion Mr L F Tremeer, a member of London Athletic Club, who had acted as starter, gave an exhibition one hundred yard race covering the distance *"in the splendid time of ten seconds amid tremendous applause"*. This was doubtless an attempt to drum up interest in the Sport, as was a whole page article in the *Kingstonian* of 1910 entitled 'How to train for Sports'. It contained a number of pieces of advice among them the following: *"cycling slows down a sprinter, avoid heavy puddings and pastry of all kinds, don't drink ginger beer or water when hot, skipping is absolutely the best method of cultivating pace."* The piece concludes with an injunction not to do anything on the day before the Sports. There do not appear to have been any contests involving other schools although the *Sportsman* reported in 1901 that R G Davis won the Quarter Mile Open in the Public School Sports in the time of 53¾ seconds and G Dewar won it in 1902. Venues for the

Sports ranged from Oil Mill Lane to Hampton Wick Cricket Club and finally in 1909 to the field at the back of the School which was not a very satisfactory area.

Rowing

On the river a shortage of boats was a key factor as was the lamentable fact that at least in 1898 the older boys who were the only ones permitted to take part, maintained first that they preferred cricket and that secondly they had too much work to do to indulge in both. In the mid 1890s there was a gradual falling away in numbers. Crews continued for a while to enter the Borough Regatta as well as the domestic Regatta and some attempt was made to produce Fours. The latter raced in Classical v Modern in 1895 and as Boarders v Day Boys in 1896, but this was something of a farce since there were only twelve boarders altogether and two of their first-choice oarsmen had accidents prior to the day of the race and had to be substituted. One of the substitutes had never rowed in a Four previously. Despite this a four-oared boat was bought in 1896 and an ill-assorted pair of crews survived until the summer of 1899. By the season of 1901 entries for the Challenge Cup for single sculls were down to small single figures and in 1902 Hack alone challenged the Cup holder Davis. In 1904 there were three entrants for the

Trophies of the Rowing Club in its early years

single scull race in the Borough Regatta but two withdrew and the event was cancelled. A temporary revival occurred in 1907 when at the Borough Regatta the Inter-Schools Fours between Kingston and Tiffin's was revived after a lapse of several years. 'Stroke' dropped out through illness and the School lost but only by a third of a length. A similar race was lost two years later and the lack of boats was again deplored. In 1910 the Kingstonian records no rowing at all, save for a failure to recover the Lovekyn Cup from Tiffin's. The blame was placed firmly on the lack of *"some benefactor who will present us with a Four .... even KGS cannot expect to turn out a winning crew in a fortnight"*. Interestingly while writing on rowing matters in the Magazine mention is made of the practice in the Heats of the Sculling Races of combining *"Part i (which) is rowed or sculled, Part ii which is swum or walked as the depth of the water may serve."*

Swimming

Interest in swimming too proved fitful. Classes were sometimes held, but when it was proposed to do so in 1904 only six boys took up the offer. Here again the mid-1890s were the highpoint. Even then however only two races took place, a 150 yard Open and a 150 yard Handicap. Tradition provided for a race for juniors but there were so few entries in 1902 that it was abandoned and in 1904 there were no races at all. In the decade before the War the School entered boys a number of times in the Surrey Secondary Schools 'Swimming Association Sports. Perhaps typical of the happy-go-lucky approach was the entry in 1909 when only the divers arrived on time as the remaining swimmers were engrossed in rehearsals for the great pageant produced that year. The exception was 1907 when the School beat Tiffin's at the Borough Regatta in a team-of-five race and in the same week won the Senior Challenge Cup at the Surrey Schools meeting beating Rutlish, Tiffin's, Sutton County and Richmond County School.

The Old Boys' Hockey Club

A feature of Schools like KGS is that they spawn Associations and Sports Clubs, and when in 1892 at a meeting at the Mitre Hotel at Hampton Court, it was suggested that a hockey Club for the benefit of Old Boys be formed it was partly as a result of dissatisfaction with the way in which the Old Kingstonian Football Club was being run. A Kingston Hockey Club was formed, but as its members were also members of Hampton Wick Royal Cricket Club it was decided in the following year to change the name to Hampton Wick Hockey Club and move to the ground at Hampton Wick and use a room at the Rose and Crown for changing and its Bar for social activities. A fixture list emerged which included names like Tulse Hill, Hampstead, Southgate and Teddington which contined to form the backbone of fixture lists for the best part of a hundred years. There was a brief interlude during

1st XI Hockey in 1917 by which time the School was renowned at this sport

the Boer War and when play resumed in 1902, the School appeared on the list for the first time.

By 1907 membership had declined to the point where it was thought neces-sary to secure a long-term source of recruits and a bargain was struck with the Headmaster of the School that the Club should thereafter be called the Kingston Grammar School Old Boys Hockey Club in deference to the footballers since they bore the title 'Old Kingstonians', and that the Headmaster should be the President. Those members who were not Old Boys were offered membership without paying the subscription which was fixed at 10/6d (52p). Between 1908 and 1914 in addition to normal matches, tours were arranged to the Isle of Wight, Guernsey and Paris. On the outbreak of war a meeting was convened and having suspended operations for the duration, the assembled members went off and enlisted in the East Surreys.

CHAPTER 14

—··◆··—

*From War (1914)
to Peace (1946)*

—··◆··—

THE FIRST DECADE OF THE TWENTIETH CENTURY had seen a decline in numbers and an inevitable decline in sporting standards as a result. The tide began to turn just before the outbreak of war, numbers increasing from 74 in 1911 to 96 in 1913 and at this point it was not unreasonable to hope that with the appointment of a new, young and presumably vigorous Headmaster, a fresh spurt forward was in the offing. Indeed it was, though for the next four years despite a continuing growth in numbers the absence of active, young members of Staff meant that not much more than a holding action could be expected. There was some reduction in the number of fixtures and the temporary disappearance of Rowing in 1918. Nevertheless one very important foundation had been laid: three Houses, Lovekyn, Queen's and Walworth, were set up in 1917 (Taverner followed in 1921). With the overall increase in pupil numbers, to 280 in 1923, and 362 in 1926 came a modicum of growth in the top of the School, though the real explosion did not take place until after the Second World War. Any increase in that area was bound to be reflected in the standard of the top two sides and the Boat Club.

As with Inchbald so it was with Howse: progress depended on the triad of numbers, facilities and instructors. The House System provided a framework within which these three could work. All games plus Drill formed part of the Competition. Hockey and cricket were sub-divided so that there were matches at Senior, Intermediate and Junior level in order to bring in as many boys as possible. As things turned out the Intermediate matches, from which First Eleven players were excluded, were the least satisfactory in quality since many of the players were definitely non-specialists. Nevertheless what they lacked in skill, especially where hockey was concerned, they more than made up for in enthusiasm and disregard for their own and indeed everyone else's personal safety. As a general principle more House points were awarded for Senior than for Junior matches and there were constant arguments over this as well as over the respective merits of the different sports. It has to be said that whatever the merits of the House System and there were many, there was to be an apathy among the non-sporting elements when it came to support on the touchline.

The Field at Dinton Road

The arguments which now presented themselves for the expansion of the School's buildings and playing areas became overwhelming very quickly in the post-war years and they prevailed with the building of the Assembly Hall and some classrooms on the one hand and the purchase of a games field at Dinton Road in 1926 on the other. Here a five acre site was developed with two cricket squares and three hockey pitches of which only one was full-sized. A timber pavilion and some adjacent changing rooms were built. Not only did the new field provide a permanent home with respectable pitches and an extremely good cricket square but it enabled games to become part of the curriculum, not something which had to be fitted into after school hours. Thus each school year group went to the games field on one afternoon each week as did most of the schools with whom we were in direct competition. None could compete on anything like level terms with the big boarding schools whose arrangements enabled their boys to play organised games every afternoon, but it was a great improvement on what had been and is probably the most significant single change in the hundred years between 1880 and 1980.

The Cage

So far as hockey, and to a lesser extent cricket, were concerned a further improvement in playing conditions occured in the mid 1930s when the area at the back of the Junior building, which had gradually been losing its grass and foliage for some while, was enclosed with wire-netting, covered in *en-tout-cas* and dubbed 'The Cage'. Since there was no machinery or manpower for damping down the surface it produced a red haze in summer and the dust permeated everything. All shoes appeared to be brown ones and the combination of Cage dust and spilt milk (in the era when third of a pint bottles of milk, prescribed by government edict, were drunk at Break) is firmly implanted in the minds of those who taught there at the time; the effect on expensive red and grey blazers was catastrophic. This latter was originally introduced as a sports blazer and only came to accepted as school uniform as a result of the exigencies of the clothes rationing which was introduced during the Second World War. The Cage provided a good all-weather surface until it was allowed to fall into such a state of disrepair that pools of water and the emergence of underlying clinker led eventually to its replacement with an asphalt surface. Hockey was played on it incessantly, before school, in Break, in the lunch hour and after school, and played by a great number of boys all at once. Pick-up games were the order of the day once more than half a dozen or so had foregathered. An on the spot decision was made in the light of the affiliations of those assembled and usually adhered to as more and more boys streamed out of the classrooms to join in. Thus at one time it might be Taverner against the Rest or at another Prefects against the Rest. Some friction did intrude in the summer when intrepid groups of boys attempted to set out their stall in order to play a form of hand, or rather book, tennis but there was normally a bit of give and take. Cage sticks were essential in this frantic world of Cage hockey. Proper hockey sticks wore out in a matter of days and only sticks already so worn that they would not serve in an ordinary game were used. They were kept in racks inside the buildings and were regarded almost as communal property. In the 1970s anyone needing such an implement could usually find one in the Book Room where the Master in Charge of hockey kept a supply: he also doled out old balls for use in the Cage. Reference has already been made to the effects of this devotion to ball control and numbers of legendary 'dribblers' emerged, though by no means all went on to play at the highest level after leaving school. This criticism notwithstanding it must be said that practice on such a surface, at a time when 'hard' hockey pitches did not exist outside the flat mud of India, was priceless.

The Increase in Staff Numbers

There was another natural corollary to the increase in school numbers in the 1920s and 1930s; more boys meant more teachers which enabled the Headmaster, if he was desirous of so doing, to people the Common Room with useful games players in greater numbers than heretofore. C A Howse did not miss the opportunity. In the immediate aftermath of War he appointed Mr J W 'Sarky' Sanders, a keen cricketer, Mr W 'Bill' Warner, a practising rower, and a little later Mr A Sharpe, a Welsh International hockey player and Mr Baker who had played cricket for Somerset. There was also Mr A D Robinson, one of a long line of Old Boys which continues to the present day, who had played both cricket and hockey while at school and also rowed in the boat; at the close of the period in 1939 another Old Boy, P R Thomas, fresh from Cambridge where he had acquired a hockey Blue joined the Staff, though the Armed Forces soon took him away. In between these two arrived Mr G E Hartley and Mr G B Forge each of whose legacies after long service are quite extraordinary. George Hartley was a natural and successful player of any game to which he chose to apply his talent. He was an active playing member of MCC and was also a good rugby player and an indecently good golfer. Geoffrey Forge was also a good cricketer and a hockey player but claimed no distinction above that of good Club standard, possibly due to a very slight physical quirk which somewhat impeded his running. Both were high-class coaches and apart from the War years exerted an enormous influence on School games for almost forty years. Geoffrey was for some years Chairman of the Committee which chose the England Schoolboys Hockey side and managed it for a time also. He had the reputation for being an extra-ordinarily shrewd judge of a player, an essential attribute at a time when side had to be selected after a short series of Trials. George Hartley was appointed as Games Master and thus held a watching brief for everything to do with games including that vital contact with the groundsman on which so much depends. He even took up a hockey stick on junior games afternoons and was to be found in the 1950s chasing down the wing when the Staff took on the First Eleven. He hated dirty cricket gear, irregular athletics kit and slovenliness of all kinds and worked on the principle that even if one was not a particularly good player at least one should try to look and behave like one. Both were committed to smart turnout and playing hard to win within the constraints of acceptable and gentlemanly conduct, a concept which in the modern sporting world seems gradually to be disappearing as the influence of money prevades the professional games and their example lamentably begins to permeate down to Club and even schoolboy level. This phenomenon would have shocked and saddened both men.

Cricket between the Wars

The development of cricket between the wars sees a considerable contrast between the state of play in the early 1920s and that of the mid to late 1930s. There was a short period immediately after the Great War during which the School had some success: in 1919 the eleven played fifteen matches, won ten of them and topped a hundred runs five times and this despite the comment that the fielding of Cochrane was *"like that of the majority .... leaves much to be desired."* By 1921 however lethargy had set in and *"very few take the game seriously ... net practice means almost nothing .... and players possess every known bad habit."* Batsmen apparently employed the windmill style of batting, played back instead of forward, their running and calling were poor and to cap it all the bowlers tried to bowl too fast and not enough energy was shown in the field. A D Robinson with a total of fifty runs from seven innings topped the averages and top score for the season was only thirty. By 1928 the *Kingstonian* commented that *"it is gratifying to notice a great increase in keenness in the School, as a result of which the standard of play has generally improved, the straight bat, or the attempt at it, being in evidence even among the weaker players."* Hundreds of spectators turned up to see the School lose by only two runs to the Old Boys. The Old Boys ran their own cricket team at this time playing some twenty matches in the season using Norbiton Sports Ground as their home venue. The School ran a Second Eleven and a Junior side in the late 1920s and these sides were well-established ten years later with a regular pattern of fixtures including St George's, Hampton, Tiffin's, Mercers, St Olave's, Brighton Grammar School and a number of touring sides like Southwark Clergy, Nomads, Jesters and of course MCC. By 1938 it was the exception if the Eleven were dismissed for under a hundred and several batsmen of above average talent scored more than five hundred runs in a season. B V Scott, who was to die tragically young soon after leaving school, achieved six hundred and forty four from fourteen innings in 1934 and was considered the best cricketer the School had ever produced. The Eleven played eighteen matches in 1939, winning eight, the Second Eleven won two out of three and the Junior Eleven played four without any success.

At the end of Summer Term each year came the MCC match, played from 1931 onwards with twelve a side under the eagle eye of F E Whitehead who raised and captained the MCC side for some twenty years. He was a stickler for protocol and did not believe that MCC should be beaten. He therefore brought a side which could be expected to contain one or two professionals from the Lords groundstaff who could generally be relied upon to get the frequently elderly gentlemen out of any trouble. The School did not win the contest until long after Frank Whitehead had disappeared from the scene. On rare occasions onlookers were intrigued to see an MCC member bowling lobs. The existence of the MCC match was at one and the same time a recognition of the standard of cricket at the School, and an incentive to improve. The knowledge that the MCC were coming focussed minds wonderfully well and in this one has to include the Master in Charge who took a suddenly excessive interest in the colour of the pads and the ability of players to return the ball somewhere in the region of the top of the stumps. Whatever the result nobody should be guilty of sloppy turnout or slovenly fielding. Afternoon games occupied the whole afternoon in the summer but only the last two periods in the winter, hockey being deemed a finite game. The School functioned as normal on Saturday mornings, in those days before the War, and Wednesday and Saturday afternoon were available for matches or other pursuits like heats for the Athletic Sports. A Cricket Week occupied the last week of the Summer Term when in addition to MCC other touring sides had pride of place; it was a social occasion with the Headmaster's wife presiding over tea.

Hockey between the Wars

Hockey too benefitted from the increase in numbers after the War and three senior elevens were soon fielded and from 1926 onwards a Fourth Eleven makes a fitful appearance. Honours came steadily at County and Divisional levels and by 1925 seven Old Kingstonians had played for their country; all but J N Macdonald (Scotland) played for England. In addition Logan and Shoveller had been selected for the Olympics. When, rather briefly, Schoolboy Internationals appeared R B Pearmund played for England Schoolboys in 1928 and G C Tryon in 1929. In addition the School produced its first hockey 'Blues' when S J Berry and P R Thomas represented Cambridge in the University Match in 1929 and 1938 respectively. All was not plain sailing however and the season 1932-1933 may be used as an

S H Shoveller the first Old Kingstonian to be capped for England at Hockey, being presented to King George V

illustration of the difficulties encountered in trying to keep up a high standard in the School with quite a broad base but a very small top echelon. At the end of the previous season all but two of the First Eleven and most of the Second Eleven had left. As a result, fielding a young and inexperienced side, the School had a poor season and lost by 1 goal to 12 against Caterham

1920. Hockey on the field at the rear of the London Road buildings, where Quadrangle and Hall now stand

The pavilion at the new Dinton Road Sports Ground, 1927

and by 3 goals to 11 against the Past. Nevertheless four sides were still fielded, though the Fourth Eleven only played once. Although there is no mention of a Junior Eleven at this point, one is recorded as playing four matches though without success the following year. At this juncture the arrival in 1932 of G E Hartley coincided with a decision to take up rugby football. Hockey would from the Autumn Term of 1933 only be played in

172

the Spring. There are arguments, no doubt urged at the time, in favour of widening the choice of games available to pupils. In respect of rugby, one powerful case is that it is possible to occupy thirty boys at any one time rather than twenty-two as in hockey or Association Football. Moreover it is said that while hockey will appeal more to those less partial to physical contact, rugby will create an opportunity for those of a heavier build and perhaps with less manual dexterity. Some cricketers will in addition argue that the hurly-burly of the rugby field will accustom cricketers to throw themselves around on a cricket field in the way that we are now becoming familiar with in the limited overs game. Without taking sides in this ongoing dispute, as difficult to resolve as is the similar argument over co-education, it must be pointed out that in this instance it was expecting too much to think that Kingston, with the human resources available to it and on a limited five acre playing field, could produce good quality sides at both rugby and hockey. That this was done at the larger Public Boarding schools ignores the facts that they had far larger areas of games field on their doorsteps and that since they took boys at the age of thirteen and not at eleven or even younger, one could not properly compare the number of boys available at a given level even if their gross totals were the same as Kingston's. It would be facile to imagine that the reputation which had been built up for prowess on the hockey field could be explained away by reference solely to the playground pick-up game, important as that was. One cannot over-estimate the contribution made by the playing of the game throughout the winter. In doing so Kingston was almost unique until the emergence of the enormous Comprehensive schools of recent times: some of them offered all possible choices through the year. Traditional smaller schools by playing rugby or soccer in the autumn condemned their hockey players to practice in the mud, frost and snow of January and February. We could indeed echo Czar Nicholas I of Russia when he praised Generals January and February for holding at bay the Allied armies in the Crimea. Moreover there is a delicious corollary: since there were no schools to play before Christmas, Kingston was forced to engage with local Clubs and although this was not always at top level it did much to toughen the School's game.

The Experiment with Rugby Football

Rugby had a brief and not very satisfactory life. It was born in 1933 and died in 1939. It was not surprising that with no background the early sides met with mixed fortunes and with some defeats in which the score was more reminiscent of bad cricket. By 1936 the hockey lobby was rumbling and the *Kingstonian* was advising hockey players to look to their laurels. The authorities took fright and decreed that hockey should again be played in the first half of the Autumn Term. With this hockey revived and of course rugby was doomed. It disappeared after the autumn of 1938 and was not revived, though in the 1970s a suggestion was made that a modicum of mini-rugby should be introduced. However on balance it was agreed that even given the greater resources provided by Ditton Field serious damage to hockey was a price not worth paying. In 1939 only a few months elapsed before those members of Staff who could coach rugby found themselves in the Forces.

The Boat Club

Progress on the river is clearly marked in this period largely as a result of the efforts of 'Bill' Warner who was one of a number of Masters to die unexpectedly whilst still so to speak in full swing. It has been noted above that rowing lived on the margin between life and death in the last century but this ceased to be the case in peacetime after 1919. Under Warner a more dedicated approach is evident from the start: within months of his arrival in 1919 the First Four was out on the river every night for three months, the Lovekyn Cup was won and a second Four entered the Borough Regatta. The School's boats were removed from Turk's boathouse and moved to the premises occupied by Kingston Rowing Club where for the first time the boys enjoyed changing facilities which included showers. House Pairs were rowed and there was talk of House Fours in the future. Tubbing took place on Saturdays throughout the winter, river conditions permitting. Thereafter crews were entered at Marlow, Egham, and the Borough Regattas, while from time to time a Second Four made its appearance, quite often contesting for the Lovekyn Cup. In the run-up to the outbreak of war in 1939 fortunes varied. The crew distinguished itself in 1936 rowing a new boat paid for by the proceeds of an appeal when not only did it win at Reading and Twickenham, and defeated Tiffin's at the Borough Regatta, but was augmented to an Eight which succeeded in beating an Old Boys' crew. However a great exodus of oarsmen left behind a much weaker Boat Club in 1937 whose only contest was for the Lovekyn Cup which they lost. Matters were not helped by the death of Bill Warner but Mr R Roebuck happily arrived and the crews again competed in 1939.

The Introduction of Boxing

Rugby was not the only innovation for which C A Howse was responsible but Fives, which was thought of as a possibility once the ground at Dinton Road was acquired, did not materialise. Boxing which had also been talked of earlier was introduced in 1930. Classes taken by the Sergeant Major were held as early as 1920 in the Hall of St Peter's Norbiton and in 1927 the Kingstonian opined that *"boxing classes are becoming an institution"*. House Points were promised if sufficient support was forthcoming. There were some thirty bouts in 1930 in a Ring set up at the East Surrey Barracks which were just across the road from the School Field. A curiosity is to be found in the competition of 1933 when the youngest contestant was apparently only eight years old (there were two

Preparatory Forms at the time) and weighed a mere 3st 6¹/₂lbs. The number of bouts varied but the average was about twenty. Once the new gymnasium was brought into use boxing was transferred. Finals usually took in all classes from 4 stone to 12 stone give or take the odd walkover. Throughout its life boxing suffered from one flaw, though one cannot say that it was frequently in evidence; this was the fact that weight not age was the determining factor in who should fight whom and thus occasionally there was the spectacle of a tall thin Senior boy fighting a much shorter, but rotund, Junior.

Other Games between the Wars

Athletics held its place but was confined to the one or two days devoted to the House Sports, held in the early days on the ground at the back of the School and later at Dinton Road. One can detect a growing air of professionalism about the proceedings with the eventual disappearance of those events which lent a specifically festive note to the proceedings. A Three-legged Race and a Wheelbarrow Race persisted into the 1930s and as late as 1936 an Under 12 Sack Race is to be found. Such events were replaced by more Relays, the

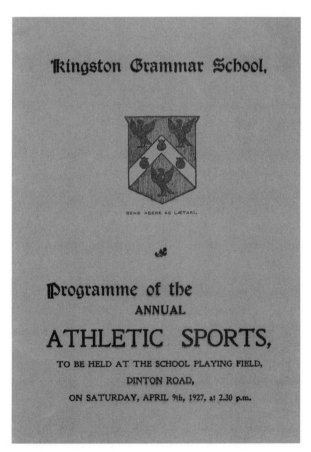

Annual Athletics Sports 1927 when Wheelbarrow Race, Three-legged Race and Tug-of-War still featured

175

Senior Weight Putt and Senior Hurdle races. Swimming, though quite well supported, suffered from poor facilities until the opening of the Coronation Baths in 1936. Although not entirely confined to the domestic competitions (which included the Mile swim in the Thames), it was limited to competitions against one or perhaps two local schools and a very restricted number of events. Whitgift and the City of London provided the opposition in the 1920s and before the outbreak of war, Emanuel and Hampton. Tiffin's were encountered to celebrate the opening of the new Baths. The Mile Swim attracted, if that is the right word, an entry of between twenty and thirty boys (thirty five in 1925) and was swum from Thames Ditton Island to Raven's Ait. From time to time the number of finishers was curtailed by unseasonable coldness of the water. Indeed in 1923 many swimmers emerged quite numb from the cold and it was usual to record those who had suceeded in completing the half-distance. Coaching classes were held under the supervision of the Baths Superintendant, Danny Emms, who went on to become something of a legend, and it was common for over a hundred certificates to be awarded. On one occasion Mr Emms gave a demonstration as an adjunct to the House Swimming in which he gave *"an imitation of a fish, swimming mistakes, bouyancy of the body, sinking like a stone, walking under water, the crab-walk swim, spinning top, wheel somersaults and ending by a performance of somersault dives from the low springboard."* Cross Country brings up the rear. The race in the 1920s still took the runners in the direction of Worcester Park and across ploughed fields. In the late 1920s about forty boys took part and this number was not exceeded until 1939 by which time the venue was Richmond Park and sixty two ran.

The Second World War

If a summary of the trials and tribulations which beset the School as a direct result of war between 1939 and 1945 is amassed it is a matter for some wonder that games was to keep going to any great extent. The retirement of the Headmaster early on, the direct effects of the Blitz, the Doodle Bugs and the V2's which had blown a sizeable hole in the Second Eleven hockey pitch at Dinton Road, the evacuation of boys at the beginning of the war which reduced overall numbers for a while to about two hundred and another scare towards the end which was not on quite the same scale, were in themselves bad enough. However to them have to be added the call-up of most of the physically active members of Staff, the death of Mr Devine, the long established groundsman, the difficulty in obtaining petrol for the motor mowers, and the difficulty in obtaining suitable cricket equipment which included items of clothing which required coupons and the problem of providing teas for matches when food was rationed. It certainly was not Business as Usual.

Into the breach left by the demands of the Armed Forces stepped existing members of staff, namely A D Robinson and J W Sanders and the two major games were kept going throughout the war. So too was Sports Day, but the others were not as fortunate: boxing disappeared for three years, swimming went altogether and the Boat Club had an uncertain time with one or two friendly races early on, being forced into the situation in 1944 where there was practice but no competitive rowing. Hockey matches were considerably curtailed and in the early days most of the matches were against Club sides: in 1942 only three matches were against other schools. The School entered the Lensbury Easter Festival in and after 1943 and by 1945 the fixture list had increased to twenty nine matches of which eighteen were won and none of the games against other schools was lost. The standard was well-maintained and of those who played in the wartime elevens four went on to play at full International level: E N Button, G W Evans, E Holmes and T R Porter. Cricket had its ups and downs, the side which took the field in 1942 being the lowest point. In that season top score was thirty nine, scored by A J Soar paradoxically in the MCC match which the School narrowly lost by eighty one runs to a hundred and five. Despite this, Soar only made fifty runs all told, outstripped by only three others of whom J Baxter's total of a mere seventy eight was the highest. With the assistance of some coaching from an old Essex professional Mr R J Carpenter who bowled very slow left-arm with a 4³/₄oz ball in the nets, the next year showed a great improvement and was distinguished by one of the most remarkable matches in the School's history. At lunch in the MCC match, the score stood at MCC eight for eight, the result of a restricted morning's play on a completely sodden wicket and outfield. The School lamentably failed to polish them off and a total of ninety five proved more than enough as the School slumped to thirty seven all out. In 1945 Alf Gover, the Surrey bowler, succeeded Carpenter as coach and this together with the survival of a Second Eleven and a Junior side provided some foundation for a post-war revival when G E Hartley reappeared.

The OK Hockey Club between the Wars

On the 25th September 1919 it was decided to revive the Hockey Club and in the following May, the Football Club then being defunct, the name was changed to the more manageable Old Kingstonian Hockey Club. The membership increased in the 1920s and by 1930 the Club was fielding five sides including an 'A' side which played against the First Elevens of some of the weaker local clubs. This latter was short-lived as was the Martlets side formed for much the same purpose after the Second World War. Fixtures increased and were usually on the basis of a home and an away match in the same season, and by the outbreak of the war Oxford and Cambridge Universities made their appearance on the list. A much-lamented weakness of the time was the absence of a second pitch at Hampton Wick so that one side had to play at Norbiton and it was difficult to foster a good Club spirit. It was in this period that a Scorpions team was formed to play Sunday matches.

177

CHAPTER 15

—··◆··—

The Post-War Era

—··◆··—

The Impact of the Enlarged Sixth Form

THE FORTY YEARS between the end of the War and the point at which the presence of girls began to have a significant impact on the number of boys available for selection for School sides was something of a golden age for the Direct Grant Grammar School. The proliferation of honours in terms of International hockey players accompanied that of Open Scholarships and is a measure of the opportunities available in the post-war. The stimuli were not applied in one sharp injection nor can they be attributed to any one change or to the overriding influence of one man, though it must be said that the desire of George Hartley to see the School achieve the highest standard in all things sporting provided a benevolent and dynamic umbrella for a good deal of this period. The most obvious single improvement, the move from the restricted Dinton Road site to the spacious and magnificently located Ditton Field, did not take place until 1965 and it was some time before teething troubles due to lack of fundamental drainage had been overcome. Meanwhile the Sixth Form had expanded rapidly in the 1950s and the pattern was established in which an annual intake of some eighty-four boys produced a school of around five hundred and sixty boys of whom about one hundred and twenty were sixth formers. The demands of the latter were to produce an expansion in the curriculum and also in the range of games available: Table Tennis and Squash were, so to speak, the partners of Biology and Russian. All this was only possible with a significant increase in Staff numbers, not far short of a fifty percent increase over the period. This enabled each sport to have its own Master in Charge and each team to have a separate Member of Staff attached to it. In the case of the hockey and cricket sides this always involved umpiring and usually coaching as well. The exceptions were the First Eleven hockey for whose matches independent umpires (many of whom were Southern Counties Umpires Association members) came to be the norm, and the First Eleven cricket who benefited from the services of a local cricket fanatic first of all and later from the services of an umpires' bureau, all of whom were extremely competent. The small sums involved were excellent value for money as they removed the Masters involved from all suspicion of partiality, a charge very frequently levelled at schoolmasters and exemplified by the comment by one umpiring what amounted to a local derby when called upon to adjudicate a ticklish lbw: *"Out! Well bowled my son!"* Moreover the master concerned could concentrate more fully on the tactical side of the game and be better primed to provide telling comments at half time or the lunch or tea interval. There was disadvantage: the more effective the leadership, the more difficult was the task of finding a replacement. In securing continuity Kingston has been extremely fortunate, a situation in no small measure attributable to the interest, acuity and diligence of successive Headmasters. One of the oddities concerning the Games Staff was that although some of those engaged in rowing or the so-called minor sports were above average performers and some, for example Rupert Stephens who started squash and John Wright who put table tennis on the map and kept it there for twenty years, were very high class performers as well as being great motivators and coaches, those who ran hockey and cricket sides were in many cases no more than moderate as performers. Their opposite numbers in other schools were frequently astonished to find that the Common Room at KGS was not crammed with international hockey players and at no time between 1945 and 1985 were there more than two members of Staff who had represented their country. When at last Richard Barker arrived to swell the ranks, one of the other two promptly gave up coaching. On the cricket side despite the fact that most of the Games Staff had played cricket at some time or another, which was certainly not true where hockey was concerned, only George Hartley could claim to be more than of average club standard. Both teams of coaches however produced a succession of high-class sides over a long period, when to lose a school match at hockey was a rarity and the cricket side held its own against other local schools, many of which had much larger numbers of senior boys from whom to select their sides.

Wednesday Afternoon Games

With the enlarged Sixth Form, Wednesday afternoon games presented a special problem never really satisfactorily solved. The whole system was based on the belief that all boys would benefit from competitive exercise in the fresh air at regular intervals. Many artistic and imaginative boys relate in their later years the subterfuges in which they indulged in order to circumvent the system. A few schools admitted defeat. A slight variant of this philosophy was once voiced by a senior KGS Classicist as follows: *"It doesn't matter what you teach them as long as they don't like it."* Thus it was necessary to provide such activities for some two hundred boys on Wednesday afternoon. Wet days in the winter are no great problem since there is no limit, subject to the Royal Parks Authority, to the number of boys who may enjoy a cross country run in

179

Richmond Park. Dry days in the winter and any day in the summer is a different matter. The Field could accommodate five games of cricket or hockey to which one may add rowers, a relatively small number of squash players, some table tennis players in the gymnasium, a few fencers in the Dining Hall, a group of swimmers in Kingston Baths and some more in other local swimming baths. This left a hard core who on their parent's affidavit indulged in such esoteric sports as horse riding, cycling or even, it was rumoured, bird watching.

The Expansion of Fixture Lists

The War had seen the disappearance of Saturday morning school and this had its effect on the pattern of fixtures. Since it was not any longer possible to combine years except on Saturdays or after school it was more productive to run 'year' sides throughout the School below fifth form level. Fifth and Sixth Forms combined for games on Wednesday afternoons and the top elevens were drawn from them. It had been the custom for exceptional players in the Fourth Year sometimes to play in the First Eleven but this practice soon yielded to academic pressure. Mid-week Year Group fixtures made an appearance and by the end of the period under discussion most of these took the form of 'A' and 'B' sides thus doubling the number able to represent the School. On Saturdays it was usual to see four cricket sides arrayed on Ditton Field while three others played on our opponents' ground. To increase further the competitive element on normal games afternoons, House Junior cricket matches were moved from their traditional Saturday mornings and played on games afternoons, and played at the bottom three age levels instead of being a composite competition in the Junior school. As time went by cricket began to come increasingly under pressure from Public Examinations and from the practice of progressively bringing back the end of the Summer Term until it now stands somewhere in the second week in July. The telescoping of the season was compounded by the practice of allowing those who had finished their Public Examinations to leave school, or at least, not to return to school once they had finished.

The expansion of both cricket and hockey fixture lists was a major feature of the period and scarcely a Wednesday or a Saturday in Term time passed without a clutch of matches. In both games the quality of the opposition improved and on the hockey field Kingston became the side against which many hockey-playing schools measure the strength of their current sides. The results may be seen in the large numbers of boys who represented their county, played in Divisional sides and achieved International status at all levels from Under 21 to Under 16 as these teams came into being. Several members of Staff were involved in the selection and management of some of these sides: Geoffrey Forge was joined on the England Schoolboys Committee by Arthur Hammond, and was Chairman of the Selection Committee for a

1973–1974 was the annus mirabilis with no less than 7 schoolboy internationals from the School

time. Gordon Evans was involved in Welsh Schoolboy hockey for a decade and more recently Jon Royce, in his spare time from coaching the School First Eleven, was also coaching the England Under 21 side. When Arthur took over running School hockey from Geoffrey Forge the transition was seamless as he continued to build on the foundations already laid. At the same time as this remarkable flowering of School hockey it must be noted that Oxbridge 'Blues' proliferated as did the number of those who represented counties and Divisions, and achieved full International honours. To date (1999) forty two Old Kingstonians have won full International honours at hockey. The latter include one Scottish, one Irish and a considerable number of Welsh amongst a predominance of English 'Caps'. Several Old Kingstonians have played for Great Britain in the Olympics and the undoubted pinnacle was reached in 1988 when Richard Dodds captained the British team which won a Gold Medal at Seoul.

Cricket 1945-1987

So far no Old Kingstonian has represented his country at cricket though two have been awarded 'Blues' and a number have played for representative sides like Young Amateurs and Surrey Colts. A few have gone on to play for County Second Elevens and one, Kevin Mackintosh, broke into the professional ranks with Surrey CCC for a short time. Apart from the top honours a measure of success in cricket was the School's performance against the MCC, while in hockey the yardstick was our performance against strong sides produced by the Past and the Hockey Association. Frank Whitehead's place was eventually taken by V J Ransom who had played for Hampshire in his day and was a Malden Wanderers stalwart who took a paternal interest in School cricket. Neither he nor his predecessor believed in giving any quarter and, faced with the prospect of being the first MCC captain to lead a defeated side, he arrived with sides of high-class amateurs laced with the odd professional from the Lords groundstaff in case of accidents. Among those whom he brought was at least one eastern potentate, Sir Leonard Hutton who crafted a memorable half-century, and his son Richard who bowled very fast and was admirably countered by P O'Neil. The pre-war habit of nets twice a week at Dinton Road became the established practice for Senior and Junior sides. The latter group also benefited from nets in a corner of the Cage where Charles Dailey resumed coaching small groups of boys abstracted from classes during

School v M.C.C. The Headmaster with the Chairman of the Governors (Maj. H J Percy M.C.) and the Captain of the M.C.C. XI (Mr F E Whitehead) 1946

the first two periods, two mornings a week, to the chagrin of many members of Staff! Cricket Week had become an established tradition though one that was to suffer from the decreasing length of the Summer Term and the increasing pressure of examinations. The period was also marked by the appearance and in due course the disappearance of the combination of School Fête and a cricket match against the Parents which enlivened a Saturday in July for many years. Another innovation was George Hartley's foundation of a Martlets cricket side composed of Old Boys, Masters and boys who played four or five matches usually in July and August against similar sides from Reid's School, Tiffin's and St George's, and touring sides like the Law Society and the Southwark Clergy. While it is invidious to single out individual sides or matches and in some ways harder to do for hockey than for cricket, it is difficult to ignore the occasion on which the newly-arrived Headmaster John Strover scored a century batting for the Headmaster's Eleven against the School in 1971 or the success of the cricket side in scoring three hundred and five for the loss of four wickets to beat Tiffin's in 1972. Over six hundred runs in one day is not bad going.

More Distant Horizons

In addition to the great overall increase in the size of the fixture list attention must be drawn to the geographical spread. Little did the pioneers of the 1920s and 1930s imagine when they visited Hamburg and Paris where their continental ventures would lead. In 1960s we entertained a cricket side from Rhodesia and the Martlets later encountered a Yorkshire Colts eleven which contained one J Birkenshaw, who on a responsive wicket demonstrated why his services were much later to be in demand by Leicestershire CC. Although it was not until much later, in 1997, that an Under 16 cricket side toured South Africa, the hockey players were swifter to take advantage of the opportunities offered by a shrinking world. The normal fixture list soon expanded to include contests with St Lawrence, Ramsgate; then came regular pilgrimages to the NPL Easter Festival, the Public Schools' Hockey Festival at Oxford at the end of the Spring Term; later on the first of a series of six visits by invitation to the Epiphany Festival of Los Reys at the palatial Polo Club in Barcelona, where KGS emerged three times as winners, and returned home bearing most impressive replica trophies. Thence to trips to Ireland, the forging of links with Holland for both hockey and cricket and most ambitious of all a trip for the U16 eleven to Australia in 1988. Another new dimension was added with the development of competitions of one kind or another for a variety of Cups at indoor as well as outdoor venues and at six-a-side as well as the more usual eleven-a-side format.

The Impact of Ditton Field

It is quite clear from what has gone before that the field at Dinton Road which

(Top) Cricket at Ditton Field with Hampton Court Palace in background
(Middle) Hockey at Ditton Field. In the background Hampton Court palace
(Bottom) Girls Hockey at Ditton Field

184

had such a beneficial effect on games in the earlier part of the century would have been quite unable to cope with the demands of the last third. The move to Thames Ditton removed the constraints imposed by a small five-acre site. Ditton Field as first acquired was much bigger and substantially more was added when the detailed plans for moving the school as a whole were being worked on in the 1970s. Such spacious accommodation to some extent obscured the absence of 'in-house' facilities such as a swimming bath and a hard, all-purpose Athletics track. Moreover Ditton Field in its early days did not provide good surfaces either for hockey or for cricket. The area had previously been little more than scrub containing a few meagre dwellings and the thinking was that if the centre of the site was raised to create a dome twelve feet above the perimeter level, it would be safe from river flooding and no drainage would be necessary. The combination of the absence of land drains and the appalling quality of the in-fill meant that until drains were later installed the whole field became waterlogged after appreciable rainfall. Many games ought not to have taken place at all and that they did was attributable only to the remarkably philosophical approach of the groundsman, Mr Newman. Grass nets were seldom of use before midsummer and Masters could be observed on games days poking the Form wickets with their shooting sticks and unearthing the most unlikely detritus, which included half bricks and seemingly endless lengths of steel wire. Gradually things improved and the construction of a hard hockey pitch hitherto a rarity on a school ground brought great benefit, although its use as tennis courts in the summer was never very successful. When much later still the area was reconstructed to take one of the new artificial carpets the School once again stole a march on the competition and tennis at last became feasible. Unfortunately so good are these new surfaces that any player expected to perform on a grass pitch has come to regard himself or herself as disadvantaged and the School is currently seeking to build another such all-weather surface.

Rowing

When one turns to Rowing the picture is equally impressive. In 1950 the Boat Club was still sharing the KRC boathouse and its equipment was woefully inadequate, a pair of Fours and the odd tub being about all that could be mustered. At this point a fairy godfather in the person of R C Sherriff, the playwright and former Captain of Boats (see Chapter 8), provided the first of a series of boats each named after one of his stage plays, the Long Sunset, Badger's Green, Home at Eight and so on, and by the time he died the tally was nearly ten. A legacy enabled the supply to continue and the building of a boathouse on the river next to Ditton Field on land which Sherriff had earlier purchased with this in mind. He had been encouraged in this by the decision to go independent in the mid-seventies, as he had always been adverse to the prospect of his contributions being subsumed by some State take-over. The

Whilst the School has yet to win at Henley, crews have collected many medals at the
National Championships

boathouse, though smaller than the School would have liked due to objections
from local residents who feared noisy gatherings, nevertheless provided an
enormous fillip for School rowing. The formation of the Sherriff Club to
enlist the support of parents, friends and well wishers also helped. In the years
before the boathouse appeared great strides had been made: House Fours
became a serious competition as did the race for the Lovekyn Cup with
Tiffin's, four Eights were put on the river of which two competed, all backed

1st Rowing VIII with their new blades

by a programme of circuit training, even if the latter was fairly restrained by the fearsome standards of today. The School regularly competed in Heads of the River at Kingston, Reading and Putney, entered various summer regattas and sent a crew to Henley. Competition from the major rowing schools, many of them boarding, proved a tough nut to crack but a succession of dedicated coaches have produced crews of quality, even if we have yet to produce a winner at Henley. Our best performance at the Tideway Head was twelfth place for the First VIII out of three hundred crews. Given the constraints of numbers and the time available it may well be that our forte in an increasingly professional sporting scene may be to produce oarsmen of distinction rather than world-beating Eights. A glimpse of the possibilities has been provided in the late nineties by the integration of James Cracknell into what promises to be a memorable Olympic Four alongside Redgrave and Pinsent.

Other Sports

Turning to what have been thought of as minor sports, competing more or less successfully with cricket, hockey and rowing for pupil interest and availability, it is clear that the dedication (sometimes amounting to fanaticism) of a particular member of Staff is often critical to their survival. In the early 1950s Water Polo attracted attention under the tutelage of Eric Thomas who was the first PE specialist to be appointed to the Staff. For some years it flourished with regular matches against other schools and producing one high-class performer in Duncan Kemp, who won a place in the Olympic Team. It proved not to have staying power. Swimming continued throughout the period with its regular Thursday afternoon visits to the Baths and Life-Saving hit the headlines as the School strove, successfully, to win the Darnell Shield. Another sport to receive stimulus from Eric Thomas was Boxing, and this survived until the public concern about the safety aspects came to the fore in the 1970s and the Headmaster, John Strover, decided it was no longer defensible. On the positive side Basket Ball, having been played in the gymnasium for very many years, has become an established part of the House Competition. Reference has already been made to the impact of John Wright, an accomplished player and International referee of table tennis. At one time the School was entering six teams in the adult Thames Valley League and numerous teams in the Surrey Schools League. Now that his influence has gone with his retirement it will be interesting to see how the sport will fare. Squash similarly owed its rise to Rupert Stephens in the days before the School possessed its own courts. It has never attracted very large numbers but has produced several players of distinction including Tom Hendry who played for Cambridge and Danny Meddings who played for Surrey. The formation of the Kingstonian Squash Club when the courts were built ensures that the sport will continue. Tennis it is true to say only properly arrived with the advent of girls twenty years ago and is still in the evolutionary stage.

Cross Country and Athletics owed much in the years following the end of the Second World War to the drive of A N Skelton, who spread his sporting talents to include hockey and cricket coaching as well. He brought a degree of professionalism to both Cross-Country and Athletics and was instrumental in moving the venue of the annual House Athletics from the doubtful grass of Dinton Road to the hard track and splendid auxiliary facilities of the London University Sports Ground at Motspur Park. Here everything was provided in first-class order and with professional assistance in such areas as hurdle erection and the maintenance of the jumping pits. Sports Day was graced by a professional starter and a suitable public address system and for a time by the sight of Jack Crump, an Old Kingstonian (then Secretary of the AAA), as he stood on the top of the steps reeling off the numbers of the finishers in the sprints with amazing speed. For sometime afterwards those Masters deputed to pick out the first four continued to gaze bemused at the heap of exhausted runners as they struggled to put names to the lucky ones and supply a correct result card for the waiting messenger to take to those compiling the House Points. A regular set of fixtures for Cross-Country and Athletics was also established.

The Great Divide

So to the last decade of the 20th century. Although co-education has affected the School's development for the last twenty-five years, the change has come about gradually, and it was not until the late 1980s that there were sufficient numbers of girls to produce sound teams at most levels. When this point was reached life of course became more difficult for the boys as their numbers fell. Clearly the worst fears of some have not been realised and the top cricket and hockey sides and the First Eight have maintained their standards. Inevitably fewer senior elevens are now fielded and the fixture lists have had to be adjusted to take this into account and block fixtures against local Club sides have gone. Moreover the strength of the age-group sides has diminished since they are selected from groups of about fifty boys instead of the traditional eighty-four. Cricket, and to a greater extent hockey, have also had to contend with other changes, mostly external, such as limited-overs matches, trophies, National Cup Competitions, indoor hockey and a proliferation of county and International demands at various levels. Kingston has responded very positively to these challenges, due partly to the thrust of tradition, partly to the use of new artificial playing surfaces and partly to the abilities and dedication of the Staff. Their influence cannot be praised too highly, especially as they also have to cope with a host of other demands on their professional expertise and time. Thus cricket, hockey and rowing owe much in this decade to Jon Royce and Peter Sheppard as previous generations did to Geoffrey Forge, George Hartley and Arthur Hammond. One visible sign of the times is that it is no longer common to see four or five sides playing hockey simultaneously on adjoining grass pitches; instead matches tend to be played consecutively on the 'astro'. Now the girls are rightly demanding that they too should share its use, another reason why the School is hoping to be able to lay down a second 'magic carpet'. The First Eleven hockey side may be justly proud of their record in the 1990s having won the Youth Under 18 Cup in 1997 for the fourth time in six years. To this must be added the Indoor Under 18 Championship in 1996. The rowers have won numerous medals at the National Schools' Championships and have won the Schools Head of the River twice, in 1993 and 1994. They have also bathed in the reflected glory of James Cracknell who was selected to represent Great Britain in the Atlanta Olympics in 1996, only to be prevented from rowing by illness. He to some extent made up for this by securing a Gold Medal in the World Championships in 1997. Other games continue to fight their own corners and their success too depends in no small measure on the abilities of the Staff involved. Thus it is still true, as it was in Inchbald's day, that a vital element in the wellbeing of school games is the Headmaster's skill in identifying and enticing the right men and women onto his Staff.

The Growth of Girls' Games

In the beginning very small numbers – in the first year (1978) there were five girls in the Preparatory Form and a handful in the Sixth form – meant that progress was painfully slow. Thanks to the efforts of Mrs P E Wisbey who was in charge of girls' PE and games from the outset, a framework of competitive games was established by the late 1980s and built on as the number of girls and female Staff allowed. The basis lay in athletics, cross country, hockey, netball, tennis and rowing where the girls operated more or less as a separate unit and other activities like table tennis where they could be more closely integrated with the boys. By 1989 the First Eleven hockey side had become Surrey Under 18 Champions, girls were playing in the Surrey Under 18 and Under 16 Elevens, two hockey teams had enjoyed visits to the Continent and the First Four had won a Silver Medal at the National School Regatta. They had clearly decided that what Kingston boys could do, so could the girls. In the 1990s success came apace: the hockey side has won the Surrey Under 18 Championship on four further occasions, the Under 16 and Under 14 sides have won their respective Surrey Cups several times, girls regularly represent Surrey and the South, while Natalie Bell was the first girl to be selected for an International Squad, namely the England Under 16's. Two 'Blues' have been achieved and Carolyn Birt was elected President of the Oxford University Women's Hockey Club. On the river the girls' Eight won the School's Head of the River in 1995 and the Women's Head in 1996. Jane Hall has distinguished herself since leaving School by winning a Gold Medal at the World Championships in 1992 as a member of the Lightweight Four, becoming Great Britain's youngest World Rowing Champion in the process.

(left) Natalie Bell played for the England Under 16 XI in 1996–7 season. She was the first girl at KGS to become a hockey international

(right) Jane Hall, left KGS in 1992. A member of GB Women's Lightweight coxless IV who won Gold at World Championships – she was Britain's youngest ever World Rowing Champion

When she and James Cracknell rowed in the World Championships in 1997 Kingston supplied more rowers than any other school. In other games standards are rising if not in quite the same spectacular way.

Retrospect

It has proved impossible in a study of this length to do justice to all, and aficionados of pursuits such as chess, fencing, shooting and soccer may well feel hard done by. Some like the fencers have fallen by the wayside, some, like those who wished to see Fives Courts built on the 'new' field at Dinton Road, never saw the light of day and some again like the chess players still flourish and can continue to boast of talented players in their ranks. The overall picture is one of constant striving to reach the highest standards and the School is proud to make its contribution towards the ideal of *mens sana in corpore sano* especially today when the part played on the sporting scene by schools in the State sector has so lamentably declined in recent years and when the worst features of professionalism so often disfigure the face of sport.

The OK Hockey Club after the 1939–1945 War

In 1940 the Old Kingstonians again stopped for war. When normal service was resumed in 1945, Arthur Sharpley was instrumental in securing the use of two pitches at Hampton Wick and the use of the pavilion for changing rooms. When five sides were playing one of them still had to be accommodated elsewhere, but the basis was there. Over the years various building projects, including a major rebuild after a fire, made the clubroom much more attractive as a social centre. Consequent on these changes the Club enjoyed a great run of successes from about 1950 onwards. Notable amongst these were the London Six-a-Side Tournament in 1958, when the Final was contested by the Old Kingstonians and a Scorpian side, and the season 1960–1961 when the First Eleven were unbeaten, a feat not performed since 1911–1912. Under the guidance of Peter Whitbread as Fixture Secretary the list was expanded to include London University and the three Services. Regular forays to Easter Festivals and several overseas trips followed.

In the last quarter of the century the Club has had to face up to several major problems and has been only partly successful in solving them. For the second time in its history the need to recruit more members necessitated a change of direction. As, increasingly, university-educated Old Boys settled away from the area, the Club bowed to pressure to go 'Open' in 1979 and a symbol of the move was to replace the Headmaster as President with an illustrious hockey player. Whether as a direct result of this change or not the fact is that a larger proportion of Kingston's hockey players now join other local clubs than had previously been the case. Lack of an Astro pitch at Hampton Wick has undoubtedly been another consideration on their minds when making such a decision, as has been their desire to play top League hockey as a foundation for a possible international career. The OK's, having at one time (1988) risen to the dizzy heights of fourth in the London League no longer compete at this level and there is no prospect of a hard pitch in a royal park. Having explored various possibilities in respect of a solution to the pitch problem, the centry draws to a close with the prospect of a deal to share the pitch at Tiffin's Girls' School, appropriate perhaps as the Club, like the School, now runs a number of Ladies' teams.

Postscript

One final thought: a record may well be in the making as no fewer than four of the current G.B. Olympic Hockey Squad training for the 2000 Olympics are Old Boys.

Appendices

—··◆··—

APPENDIX A

Headmasters of Kingston Grammar School
(until 1904 Queen Elizabeth's Grammar School, Kingston)

1564	Reverend John Laurence M.A., St John's, Cambridge
1565	Roger Foster M.A., St John's, Cambridge
1573	Reverend Stephen Chatfield M.A., Cambridge
1584	Simon Kirkton
1588	Justinian Whiting M.A., Corpus Christi, Oxford
1596	Mr Correr
1599	Reverend William Denman M.A., Clare, Cambridge
1599	Richard Hancoke B.A., Gloucester Hall, Oxford
1609	William Beeley M.A., Corpus Christi, Oxford
1613	Ambrose Richmond M.A., Oxford 1602, M.A., Cambridge 1607
1620	Reverend Henry Panton M.A., Queen's, Oxford
1622	Reverend Thomas Tyroe B.A., Queen's, Oxford
1626	Robert French M.A., Gloucester Hall, Oxford
1637	William Burton M.A., Gloucester Hall, Oxford
1658	William Cooke M.A., Oxford
1661	Mr Bowerman
1663	Dr Hooker
1663	Charles Parkhurst
1685	Thomas Rowell, St John's, Cambridge (degree not known)
1699	Reverend Robert Comyn M.A., Magdalen, Cambridge
1702	Reverend Henry Winde (University not known)
1730	Reverend Samuel Heming M.A., Queen's, Oxford
1732	Reverend Richard Wooddeson M.A., Magdalen, Oxford

1772	Reverend John Griffiths M.A., Jesus, Oxford
1780	Reverend Hugh Laurents, Pembroke, Oxford (degree not known)
1797	Reverend Thomas Wilson, M.A., Sidney Sussex, Cambridge
1832	Reverend John Stansbury M.A., Magdalen, Oxford (DD 1844)
1849	Reverend William Rigg, M.A., Pembroke, Cambridge
1883	Reverend William Elliot Inchbald M.A., Clare, Cambridge
1904	Edward Norman Marshall M.A., St John's, Cambridge
1905	Ernest Alfred Stowell B.A., Queen's, Oxford
1913	Charles Aubrey Howse M.A.,Clare, Cambridge
1941	E W James, M.Sc., Victoria University, Manchester
1950	Percy William Rundle M.A., King's, Cambridge
1970	John Anthony Strover M.A., Trinity, Oxford
1977	Sidney James Miller M.A., Jesus, Cambridge
1987	Anthony Browning Creber, M.A., London
1991	C Duncan Baxter M.A., Trinity, Oxford

NB For the period up to 1800, the information about Masters is taken primarily from Manning and Bray's *History of Surrey* (1804). They collated the details from lists of the Masters in *"the book in which the account is kept of the revenues of the School, but their Christian names are frequently wanting, nor do the dates of their appointments often appear, or whether the new Master comes in on death or resignation"* (p. 358).

APPENDIX B

Second Masters/Deputy Heads

Mr Ginn	– 1883
E Docker M.A., Cambridge	1883 – 1901
C E Hudson M.A., Cambridge	1901 – 1903
C H Ross B.A., Cambridge	1903 – 1907
R H Cocks B.A., Oxford	1909 – 1914
H L White M.A., Cambridge	1916 – 1920
E W James M.Sc , Victoria, Manchester	1921 – 1941
H W A Wadley M.A., Cambridge	1941 – 1947
J W Sanders B.A., London	1947 – 1953
A D Robinson M.A., Cambridge	1953 – 1962
H J Ellis M.A., Cambridge	1962 – 1967
G E Hartley M.A., Cambridge	1967 – 1973
G W Evans B.A., Oxford	1973 – 1987
R J Sturgeon M.A., Cambridge	1987 – 1995
E M C Hivers B.A., York	1995 – 1997
J R Hind M.A., Cambridge	1997 –

APPENDIX C

School Captains

Reverend Elliot Inchbald introduced a system of School Prefects in 1886, and the first recorded School Captain (or Senior Prefect as known until 1923) was A R A Everingham. The year shown in the list below is that of appointment.

Date	Name	Date	Name
1887	A R A Everingham	1924	J C Greig
1888	A J Marsh	1925	J O Fowler
1890	C W Fisher	1926	S J Berry
1891	P Hide	1928	V Packer
1893	P G T Logan	1929	J G Rae
1894	H G Ford	1930	A C Bailey
	S G Marsh	1931	H R Stimson
1895	C W C de Boinville	1932	K L Kelly
1896	B E Sanson	1933	S J Bonney
1897	C F Ford	1934	P R Thomas
1898	G Logan	1935	B Crowther
	S H Shoveller	1936	E W Rolt
1899	C H S Bennet	1937	F H Jones
1900	C S Burge	1938	D P Durham
1903	G Dewar	1940	A Kirby
	C J Stevenson	1941	R H James
1904	N Marston	1942	P E G Bates
1905	D W Scogins	1943	E Holmes
1907	H L Starkey	1945	E N Button
1908	B J W Nicholas	1946	N D Cowderoy
1910	E Watson	**1947**	**B D Dance**
1912	G H Stoodley	**1948**	**B D Dance**
1913	A B Winser	**1949**	**R D Finlay**
1915	H D Scogings	**1950**	**R D Finlay**
1917	R G Alderson	**1951**	**M J Rowbottom**
1920	S H Lewis	**1952**	**B M Virgin**
1922	A D Robinson		
1923	F L Dodman		

Date	Name	Date	Name
1953	M Cowan	1978	R J Welsh
1955	N T Roberts		D M Allen
1956	M R Colmer	1979	A J Puttock
1957	M J Rustin	1980	M C Hussey
1958	M E Drummond		J L Peak
1959	A P Conway	1981	R J McIntyre
1960	C Bailey	1982	R J P Kerr
1961	G J Hunt		D E Jenkins
1962	P R Allen	1983	M W Bull
1963	B C Harris	1984	S R Ellingham
1964	R P H Foster	1985	D M Trickey
1965	T Thomas	1986	A W Spence
1966	G W Bishop	1987	C Waters
1967	A R Jones	1988	B J Bladon
1968	R L Barker	1989	C A Williams
1969	B R Martin	1990	V J Lipscomb
1970	J P H Fine	1991	N J Griggs
1971	R V Natkiel	1992	O M Foa
1972	K S Bates	1993	S N Burmester
1973	M K Lunt	1994	C W Ross
1974	R I Cheetham	1995	C Birt
1975	P J Dainty	1996	G E Aitken-Davies
1976	C J McKay	1997	D P Simon
1977	M Gallimore	1998	O Thomson
	R D A Dodds	1999	J J Alexander

APPENDIX D

Hockey Internationals

The following 42 Old Kingstonians gained full International Colours, playing for England unless otherwise stated. The date shown is the year an International Cap was first awarded.

1902	S H Shoveller	
1906	G Logan	
	N T Nightingale	
1913	J H Fawcett	
	W R Matthews	
1925	H J Still	
	J N Macdonald	(Scotland)
1933	S J Berry	
1936	W D Chambers	(Ireland)
1947	P Whitbread	
1948	R Grove	
1949	E Holmes	
1950	E N Button	
	G W Evans	(Wales)
1951	T R Porter	
1953	D L Wilson	(Scotland)
1956	C H Dale	(Wales)
	M O H Doughty	
1957	P B Austen	
1958	P A Douty	
1959	D R Miller	
1960	D J Prosser	(Wales)
1961	T N Snow	(Wales)
1962	R B Constable	
1965	H D V Bebb	(Wales)
	R P Meeres	(Wales)
	M J B Crowe	
1970	H Morgan	
	R L Barker	
1971	P C Freitag	
	A P Davies	(Wales)
1973	D R Hulbert	

1974	A A Jeans	(Wales)
1975	A Western	(Wales)
1977	G D Featherstone	
1978	M Gallimore	
	R D A Dodds	
	G N Francis	
1982	S J Rees	(Wales)
1983	A N Diamond	
1995	G T Fordham	
1996	D J Hall	
1997	B S Garrard	

APPENDIX E

The Text of the Royal Letters Patent of 1st March 1561 Founding the School

ELIZABETH by the grace of God Queen of England, France and Ireland, Defender of the Faith, etc., to all to whom these present letters shall come, greeting. Know ye that at the humble petition of our beloved subjects the Bailiffs and free men and inhabitants of our town of Kingeston-upon-Thames in our county of Surrey for a grammar school within the aforesaid Parish of Kingeston in our said county of Surrey, to be erected and established for the training (and) instruction of boys and youths, by our special grace and of our certain knowledge and of our mere motion, we will, grant and ordain for us and our heirs that henceforth there be and shall be a grammar school to endure for ever in the said town of Kingeston-upon-Thames, which shall be called the free grammar school of Queen Elizabeth, for the education, training and instruction of boys and youths in grammar. And we erect create and ordain declare and found by these presents that school, to continue for ever under one Pedagogue or Master and on Subpedagogue or Undermaster. And that our aforesaid intention may the better take effect and that the lands, tenements, rents, revenues and other profits granted, assigned and apportioned for the upkeep of the aforesaid school may be better governed for the continuance of the same, we will, grant and ordain for us and our heirs that the two Bailiffs of the aforesaid town for the time being shall be and shall be called governors of the possessions, revenues and goods of the said school commonly called or to called the free grammar school of Queen Elizabeth in the town of Kingeston-upon-Thames in the county of Surrey. And therefore know ye that by these presents we have assigned, chosen nominated, constituted and declared, and we assign, choose, name constitute and declare by these presents that our well-beloved William Matson and George Snellinge now Bailiffs of the aforesaid town of Kyngeston-upon-Thames shall be and are the first and present governors of the possessions, revenues, and goods of the said free grammar school of Queen Elizabeth in the town of Kingeston-upon-Thames in the county of Surrey, to execute and occupy that office well and faithfully, from the date of these presents, as long as they shall happen to be in the office of Bailiff of the aforesaid town of Kyngeston. And that the same governors be and shall be in deed fact and name henceforth one body incorporated and politic for ever, by the name of the governors of the possessions, revenues and goods of the free grammar school of Queen Elizabeth, incorporated and erected in the town of Kyngeston-upon-Thames in the county of Surrey. And we incorporate by these presents William Matson and George Snellinge as Governors of the possessions, revenues and goods of the free grammar school of Queen Elizabeth in the town of Kingeston-upon-Thames in the county of Surrey. And by these presents we create, erect, ordain, make, constitute and declare actually and fully the body corporate and politic to endure for ever by the same name. And we will and by these presents grant for us, our heirs and successors that the same Governors of the possessions, revenues and goods of the free grammar school of Queen Elizabeth in the town of Kingeston-upon-Thames in the county of Surrey shall have a perpetual succession and by the same name are and shall be persons fit and capable in the law to hold, receive and acquire from us the Chapel, houses, buildings, rooms, structures, rents, reversions, possessions, revenues and hereditaments written and specified below, and other lands, tenements, possessions, revenues and hereditaments whatsoever from us or from any other person or other persons whatsoever.

[There follows a detailed list of the Chapel premises.]

And further of our more ample grace we have given and granted and by these presents do give and grant to the aforesaid Governors all the issues, rents, revenues and profits of the aforesaid chapel and of all the other premises from the feast of Saint Michael the Archangel last past. The same Governors to have as of gift without account or rendering, paying or doing some other in like manner to us, our heirs of successors in any way. And further we will and grant for us, our heirs and successors to the aforesaid Governors and their successors that henceforth they should have for ever a common seal for their aforesaid business expressed and specified in these our letters patent whether touching or concerning any parcel of it. And that the Governors themselves in the name of the Governors of the possessions, revenues and goods of the free grammar school of Queen Elizabeth in the town of Kingeston in the county of Surrey may plead and be impleaded, defend and be defended, answer and be answered in whatsoever courts and places and before whatsoever judges and justices in whatsoever causes actions affairs suits plaints pleas and demands whatsoever and of whatever nature or condition they be. And further of our more ample grace we have given and granted, and by these presents do give and grant for us our heirs and successors to the aforesaid present Governors of the aforesaid school and their successors that they and their successors with the advice of the Bishop of Winchester for the time being should have full power and authority to nominate and appoint a Master and Undermaster of the aforesaid school as often as the same school shall be without a Master and Undermaster. And the Governors themselves with the advice of the aforesaid

Bishop of Winchester for the time being should from time to time make and have the power and authority to make suitable and beneficial statutes and ordinances in writing concerning and touching the rule, government and direction of the Master and Undermaster and scholars of the aforesaid school for the time being, and of the stipend and salary of the same Master and Undermaster, and other things appointed and to be appointed touching and concerning the same school and the ordering, government, preservation and disposition of the rents and revenues for the maintenance of the same school. Which statutes and ordinances thus to be made we will, grant and by these presents do order to be inviolably observed henceforth for ever.

....

In witness whereof we have caused these our letters to be made patent. Witness myself at Westminster on the first day of March in the third year of our reign.

> By writ of privy seal and given by the aforesaid authority of parliament. Inrolled in the office of me John Thompson Auditor.

Select Bibliography

—··◆··—

The abbreviation KLHR is used for the Kingston Local History Room, North Kingston Centre where Borough Archives, Census Returns, and local newspapers back to the 19th Century may be studied.

SECTION I – ORIGINAL SOURCES

Census Returns, 1841 onwards	KLHR
The Church Brief of 1585 (A national appeal for funds to build a new School)	School Library
Elizabeth I, Charters of 1561 and 1564	KLHR/School Library
Games Committee Minutes (various from 1910 onwards)	School Library
GIBBON Edward, *Memories of My Life*, posthumously 1796	
Governing Bodies (Minutes of meetings 1872 onwards)	KLHR to 1977 School thereafter
Inspectors' Reports (1865, 1903, 1914, 1924, 1934, 1958 and 1995)	School Library
Kingston Endowed Schools Trust – Scheme 1872	KLHR
LOVIBOND Edward, *Poems on Several Occasions* 1787	
School Accounts, 1674 onwards	KLHR
School Pageant Programme July 1909	School Library/KLHR
School Statutes and Ordinances 1671 and 1832	KLHR
WINDE Henry, Reverend, His Petition to Bishop of Winchester, 1725	School Library

SECTION 2 – SECONDARY SOURCES

The *Annual Register* (the School Magazine 1883 to 1904)	School Library
BELLARS M, *Kingston Then and Now*, 1977	

BIDEN W D, *History and Antiquities of the Ancient and Royal Town of Kingston upon Thames*, 1852

BRAYLEY E W, *Topographical History of Surrey*, 1852

BUTTERS S A, *The Book of Kingston*, 1995

COWAN M C, *History of the School* (A series of 6 articles in The Kingstonian 1953–55)

The Dictionary of National Biography, 1921 reprint

FINNY W E Dr, "Lovekyn's Chantry Chapel and Free Grammar School", 1933 Typescript — School Library

HEALES A (Major), *Early History of the Church of Kingston upon Thames . . . of the Free Chapel of St Mary Magdalene, and the Free Grammar School of Queen Elizabeth*, 1883

JAMES Robert H, "History of Kingston Grammar School". Unpublished typescript — School Library

The Kingstonian, (the School Magazine 1907 onward 1912-1917 missing) — School Library

MANNING O and BRAY W, *History and Antiquities of the County of Surrey* 1804–1814, (pp. 350–58)

MERRYWEATHER F S, *Half a Century of Kingston History*, 1887

The *Red and Grey* (Unofficial School Magazine 1950-1960) — School Library

ROOTS G, *The Charters of the Town of Kingston upon Thames*, 1797

RUNDLE P W, "Kingston Grammar School – An Outline History" (A short memoir prepared for the Royal Visit in 1961) — School Library

SAMPSON JUNE, *The Story of Kingston*, 1972
——*Hidden Kingston*, 1975
——*All Change, Kingston, Surbiton and New Malden in the 19th Century*, 1985

Surrey Comet, issues from 1860 onwards deal with School — KLHR

Surrey Comet, Illustrated Brochure "The Queen Came to Kingston – 24th March 1961" — School Library

Victoria County History Vol II, 1905, (pp. 151–64)

WAKEFORD JOAN, *Kingston's Past Rediscovered*, 1990

Details of all material relating to the School which is held in the Borough Archives are in *Royal Borough of Kingston upon Thames – Guide to the Borough Archives* published 1971. Available at KLHR.

Index

———••◆••———

Note: References to illustrations are in *italics*.

209